BUILDING FOR THE FUTURE

The Story of Consumers Energy, 1886-2016

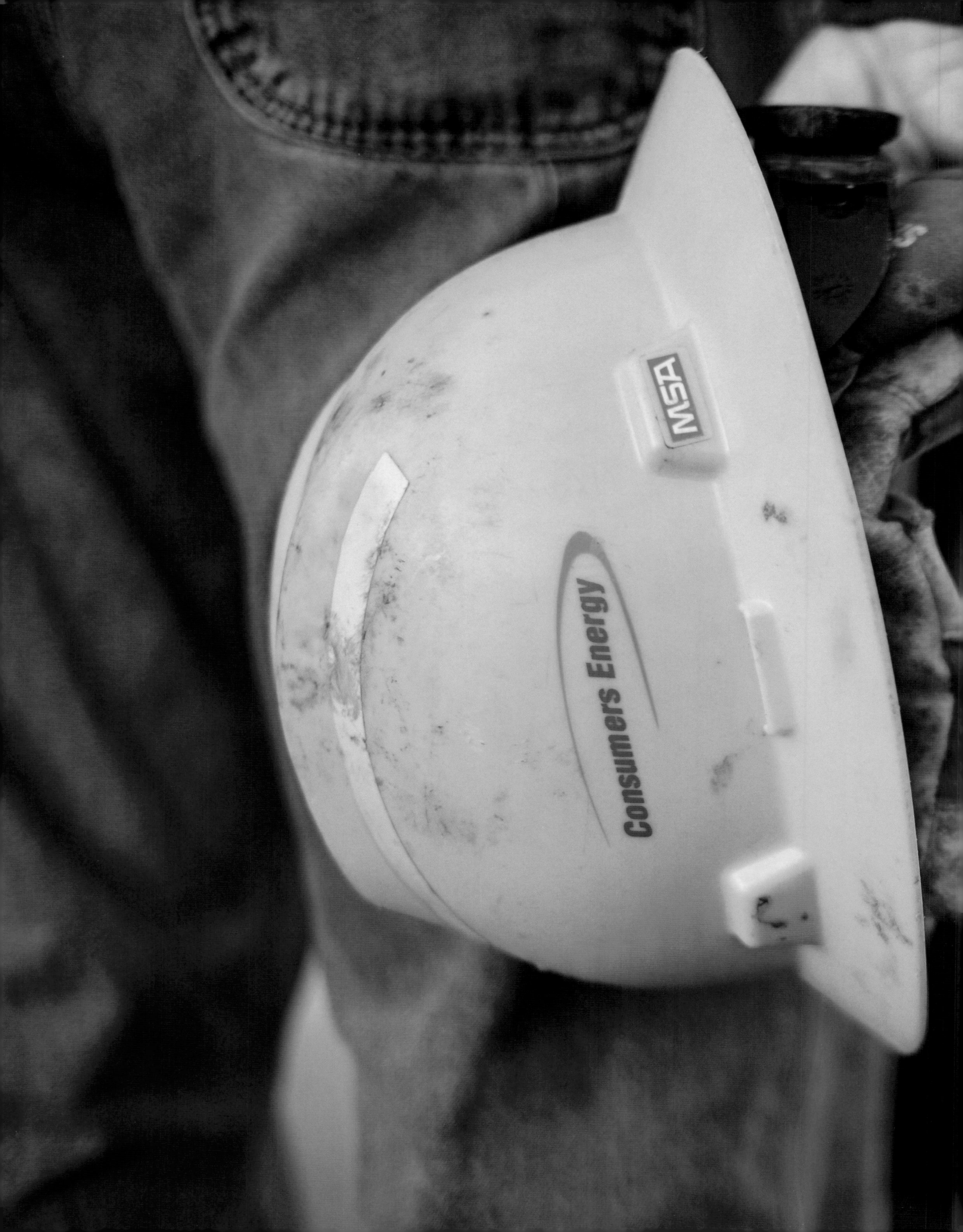
MSA
Consumers Energy

Building for the Future

THE STORY OF CONSUMERS ENERGY, 1886-2016

by Gina Shaw

ESSEX PUBLISHING GROUP, INC.

Produced and published by Essex Publishing Group, Inc.,
St. Louis, Missouri.
www.essexink.com

Book design by Clare Cunningham Graphic Design
Cover design by Clay McAndrews, Consumers Energy

Library of Congress Catalog Card Number: 2016961989

ISBN: 978-1-936713-11-0

First Printing: February 2017

Any trademarks in this book are property of their respective owners.
Lake Winds Energy Park® and Cross Winds Energy Park® are trademarks of CMS Energy Corporation.

All images courtesy of Consumers Energy, with the following exceptions:

Page 15 top: Courtesy of the Youngdahl family
Page 57: Courtesy HistoricImages.com
Page 132: Courtesy Moran Iron Works

A special thank-you to photographer Tom Gennara, whose work is seen throughout this book.

Table of Contents

Chapter 1: The Big Battery   8

Chapter 2: "The Lights Is Workin'!"   18

Chapter 3: Building Boom   42

Chapter 4: Count on Us   62

Chapter 5: Promise and Peril   78

Chapter 6: From the Brink   100

Chapter 7: Renewable   124

Acknowledgments/About the Author   150

Company Leaders   151

Timeline   152

Index   155

The relatively simple technology behind the Ludington Pumped Storage Facility enables it to hit peak production in minutes, harmonizing customer demand with electric output on a moment's notice. An essential part of Consumers Energy's balanced energy portfolio, Ludington can respond nimbly to peaks and valleys in energy demand.

1: The Big Battery

"While most utilities are trying to figure out what went wrong last week, Consumers Energy Co. will spend just as much time figuring out what went right," *Crain's Detroit Business* wrote after the extensive August 2003 blackout. A well-designed system, including backup from Ludington, helped ensure that only 100,000 of Consumers Energy's customers lost power statewide. The company's crews restored fully half of those customers' electricity within hours, while much of the Eastern Seaboard waited days for power to return.

A ugust 14, 2003, dawned bright and hot across most of the Eastern and Midwestern United States. The nation's electrical grid faced its usual heavy late-summer demand, as people in homes and offices across the region switched on fans and cranked up the air conditioning.

Around midday, a bad data reading in a power flow monitor on the Midwestern grid triggered a cascade of events that rapidly spun out of control. An Ohio power plant shut down, a major transmission line failed and, just after 3 p.m. in northern Ohio, a 345-kilovolt power line tripped when it overheated and sagged into an untrimmed tree.

An outage of that kind is typically an easily corrected, minor problem, but software in the Ohio utility's control center failed to detect it, and soon two more lines failed. Controllers

at the Ohio utility, intent on understanding their system's outages, did not inform system controllers in neighboring states. Then the dominoes began to fall.

Line after line tripped in Ohio and Michigan, and, with major arteries blocked, the grid's operator tried to balance the supply of electricity with demand, routing power from one part of the grid to another. Two large power surges ensued, knocking out more transmission lines and power plants, and spreading the blackout northward and eastward in a hurry.

By 4:15 p.m., at least 12 major transmission lines had failed, segments of the grid had disconnected from one another, 256 power plants had shut down, and some 55 million people in eight U.S. states (including Michigan and Ohio) and Canada were without electricity.

The second most widespread blackout in history was underway, and in some remote areas it lasted nearly a week.

"THE UNITS GROANED"

The first Bill Schoenlein heard of the blackout was around 4:10 p.m. He was manager of the Ludington Pumped Storage facility, a "peaking" hydroelectric plant that can kick on at a moment's notice when energy demand is extreme. Situated on the eastern shore of Lake Michigan, Ludington was completed in 1973 as a joint venture between then-Consumers Power and Detroit Edison. Today, the plant is operated by Consumers Energy, which provides power to more than 6.8 million homes and businesses throughout Michigan's 68 Lower Peninsula counties. Consumers Energy is Michigan's

Every day, Consumers Energy, whose headquarters is in Jackson, brings electricity and natural gas to more than 60 percent of Michigan's households and businesses.

Consumers Energy understood the importance of natural gas from its earliest days, when founder William A. Foote added gas companies to his growing electricity business. Today, the company's longtime position in natural gas—such as the Howell natural gas field, shown here—allows it to take advantage of the current cost benefits of gas, keeping prices low.

largest power company and the fourth-largest combination utility in the United States.

Schoenlein was at a meeting 90 minutes away from Ludington when word came that one of the power surges had caused an interconnection in central Michigan to exceed its emergency rating—and conditions were rapidly deteriorating.

"Detroit Edison's down to zero," he was told, and the message was clear: Detroit Edison (DTE Energy), Michigan's second-largest utility, wasn't generating any electricity at all except at Ludington; a lot of Michigan was dark, and keeping the lights on in the state would be up to Consumers Energy. Schoenlein's plant was a critical link in the national grid, and he knew that if Ludington went down, the situation would become much worse.

Anxiously, he picked up the phone.

"I called the plant and asked how things were going," he recalls. "An operator named Craig said calmly, 'Everything's fine. The units groaned when the blackout hit, but they kept going.'"

At the turn of a switch at Ludington, water had surged downward through huge pipes from a 27 billion-gallon reservoir on a bluff overlooking Lake Michigan. Three hundred and sixty-three feet downhill from there, the water turned six reversible-pump turbines, each more powerful than an aircraft carrier engine, generating electricity. Rated at approximately 450,000 horsepower, the turbines typically generated 312 megawatts of power apiece, or about 1,872 megawatts in total. Five of the turbines were in service that day, and Schoenlein found out later that, as the blackout rolled through, each unit had produced 400 megawatts, much higher than anyone had expected.

About a dozen other power plants in Michigan had shut down, including all three coal-fired units at Consumers Energy's J.R. Whiting complex on the Lake Erie shore in southeastern Michigan, and one unit each at its J.H. Campbell plant near Holland and D.E. Karn/J.C. Weadock coal complex at the mouth of the Saginaw River. Ludington's turbines continued to turn, however.

"We pumped the reservoir up as full as we could, right to the limit, so we could produce as much as we could," John Hutchinson, the plant's operations supervisor, told the *Ludington Daily News*. "We're prepared to provide as much power as we can, and we have reduced our internal loads and curtailed maintenance."

By then, the blackout had reached as far south as Baltimore, as far east as Massachusetts and as far north as southern Ontario. With the Empire State Building standing dark and New Yorkers climbing out of stranded subway cars, and with most of Detroit's residents doing without air conditioning, lights and in some cases drinking water, Ludington's employees worked through the night.

"Those units fought against decline in frequency and helped support the grid from further failing," says Consumers Energy Chairman of the Board John Russell, who was president and chief executive officer of the company's electric business at the time of the blackout. "Ludington can't be given all the credit, but it was an essential resource that helped the grid provide energy and kept the blackout from proceeding further."

Thanks to Ludington (considered one of the world's largest "batteries"), the company's baseload coal generation plants and the Palisades nuclear plant, Consumers Energy was able to quickly send enough power into its system to keep the grid alive, prevent the rest of its plants from shutting down and offer the Midwest Independent Transmission System Operator (MISO) a largely functioning network through which to route power as the grid was being repaired elsewhere. Because of the electricity generated by Ludington and the company's 23 other hydroelectric and fossil generating units that stayed online, Consumers Energy was able to continue serving most of its customers and help reboot a powerless nation.

By the time the blackout ended, only 2.3 million of Michigan's 10 million households and businesses had lost power—and the vast majority of those whose lights stayed on were Consumers Energy customers.

A "Family" Business for 130 Years

Consumers Energy has been a family business from the beginning, when it was built by brothers W.A. and J.B. Foote. Today, countless other teams of siblings, parents and children, grandparents and grandchildren continue to make Consumers Energy their own family's legacy.

If there were a Guinness record for most family members working at the company, it would probably be held by the Barrett family. Patriarch Francis W. "Frank" Barrett started working in the Tabulating Department for what was then Consumers Power in its old main building on Michigan Avenue in 1952. He retired in 1987 as the director of personnel and safety for the South Central Region.

Multiple generations of Barretts followed their dad's lead into the Consumers Energy fold. Of the Barretts' nine surviving children, seven have worked at Consumers Energy at some point in their lives. Three are now retired, and three still work for the company.

"We've counted at least 16 family members who've worked at Consumers Energy so far—our siblings, sisters- and brothers-in-law, children, nieces and nephews," says Frank's son Andy Barrett, a purchasing and supply chain advisor, "and that doesn't include extended family that work here."

Andy's sister, Laurie (Barrett) Harris, a business support consultant who's worked for the company since 1978, says, "Witnessing our

The Barrett family. Back row, left to right: Kevin Harris, Kris Kloack, Coley Kloack, Mike Barrett, Debbie Barrett, Pete Barrett. Middle row, left to right: Tyler Harris, Laurie Harris (holding picture of Frank Barrett), Shad Warner. Seated: Teresa Kloack, left, and Andy Barrett.

dad's passion and dedication to his work with Consumers Power gave us the motivation to pursue a career with the company."

Today, Harris' two sons, Kevin and Tyler Harris, are also Consumers Energy "legacies."

"We are spread across the state from east to west," she says. "We've had family members working as union and non-union employees, and as interns with summer jobs. My nephew, Coley Kloack, is a journeyman lineworker in Jackson and an instructor at the Marshall Training Facility, teaching new generations of lineworkers."

Andy's daughter, Brooke, just turned 10 this year, and he says she's already planning on working for Consumers Energy someday.

"We're all very proud to wear the colors," he says. "We couldn't be more honored by the legacy our dad left for us with Consumers Energy."

Two other Consumers Energy "patriarchs" are nuclear scientists Russell Youngdahl and Bill Kessler, who worked together in the early 1970s, helping Consumers Energy seek licensure for the Midland nuclear plant. Now retired, the two men share the pride of seeing later generations of their families working for the company they helped grow.

Two of Youngdahl's granddaughters, Lauren Youngdahl Snyder and Leslie

Youngdahl, work for Consumers Energy. Lauren is executive director of customer experience and marketing strategy, and Leslie is a senior communications consultant.

"Every time I see them, I ask, 'How's my company doing?'" says Youngdahl, who retired in 1983 as executive vice president in charge of energy operations. "They're nice enough that they like to talk company business with me, too. They've even called me and asked me

some questions sometimes!"

Kessler started his career with Westinghouse, testing reactors in Idaho and training Navy personnel to operate the first nuclear-powered seafaring vessels, the submarine USS Nautilus and the aircraft carrier USS Enterprise. With the exception of a break during which he worked for Gilbert/Commonwealth, an offshoot of former Consumers Energy parent company Commonwealth & Southern, Kessler spent the rest of his career at Consumers Energy before retiring in the late 1990s.

Two decades later, Kessler was overjoyed when his daughter Patti Poppe told him in 2011 that she would be joining his beloved company as vice president of customer operations. But he was more than a little shocked four years later, when Poppe told him she had been named as successor to Consumers Energy President and CEO John Russell, who would retire in 2016.

"Holy mackerel, Patti!" was all Kessler could say.

Poppe says, "We shed a little tear wishing my mom was still here with us to celebrate. Life has taken me many places, but it sure feels good to be home at Consumers Energy."

A lot of families know just how she feels.

Proudly serving
MICHIGAN for
125
YEARS

Ludington could easily do it again, Schoenlein says: "If all the power in Michigan went out right now, our on-site diesel generator could help start the #2, #3 or #5 turbines, and they could start the rest."

A MICHIGAN UTILITY

Today, the Ludington Pumped Storage Facility is a vital part of a diverse, evolving portfolio of resources deployed by Consumers Energy to bring electricity and natural gas to its customers. It also plays an important role in the company's expanding renewable energy strategy, and it stands as a premier example of Consumers Energy's commitment to energy innovation and reliable service to the people of Michigan.

Consumers Energy began in 1886 as a collection of small, separate electric and gas businesses in several cities in Michigan's Lower Peninsula. These eventually came together under the name of the Jackson Electric Light Works. In the ensuing century, the company that became Consumers Energy built dozens of hydroelectric plants along with a dozen coal-fired and two oil-fired generating plants. It opened two nuclear plants, ultimately decommissioning one and selling the other. It became Michigan's largest natural gas company, with the largest gas storage system in the state and one of the largest in the nation.

Every day, Consumers Energy, headquartered in Jackson, brings electricity and natural gas to more than 60 percent of Michigan's households and businesses. It also plays a major part in shaping U.S. energy policy and setting new standards for the industry in energy efficiency, development and deployment of new technologies, and stewardship of natural resources.

Over its 130 years in business, Consumers Energy has survived several disastrous turns of fortune, some due to market forces outside its control and others because of strategically ill-advised decisions about where to focus its attention and invest its resources. After coming back from the brink of bankruptcy more than once, Consumers Energy is stronger because of the hard lessons learned, John Russell says.

"What sets Consumers Energy apart is our focus on breakthrough thinking," Russell says. "Ten years ago, we were coming out of some desperate times and were still in a funk of daily crisis. We realized that if we were to succeed, we had to decide what we were going to succeed at."

Consumers Energy unwound a complex trading operation, sold overseas and out-of-state power plants it had acquired, and got out of the nuclear generation business. It made the decision to simply be a utility, focused exclusively on Michigan.

"We had to focus on operational excellence—what it means to be the very best utility we can be," Russell says. "That means we have to do a lot of things: ensure safety, affordability, reliability and sustainability, and do them all well. We have to ensure that our service is best in class and that it provides value to the customers. Some companies will sacrifice one element of excellence for another, but we've learned you can't do that. You have to put it all together."

Those lessons have paid off.

In 2014, Consumers Energy was named one of the top 15 sustainable energy providers in the world, received the Edison Electric Institute's Index Award for top cumulative shareholder return among electric companies nationwide, and received the second-highest customer satisfaction rating among large Midwest utilities in J.D. Power's customer satisfaction survey.

Consumers Energy retired seven of its oldest fossil-fuel generating plants, including the J.R. Whiting plant pictured below, in April 2016 and made a major commitment to upgrade emission controls at its remaining fossil plants.

In 2016, Consumers Energy experienced the safest year in its history. The company was able to commit nearly $200 million to upgrade more than 88 miles of natural gas infrastructure throughout Michigan, and it made good on a promise to increase its spending with businesses in the state by $1 billion. In a study by Cogent Reports, Consumers Energy was named one of the most trusted utility brands of the year.

A FAMILY ATMOSPHERE

It's not surprising, then, that Consumers Energy's more than 7,300 employees take great pride in what they do and typically enjoy long, rewarding careers with the utility. Though the company's roots may date to the 19th century, its values are progressive—team-oriented, collaborative and unpretentious.

"I started working at the J.C. Weadock generating plant as a co-op student when I was 17 years old," says Generation Supply Chain Contract Analyst Debbie Lupo. It was a stepping stone to a 36-year career at Consumers Energy.

"The older employees helped me and made me feel like a part owner. We were all family. I wouldn't have what I have today without Weadock and Consumers Energy."

Consumers Energy began with the vision of a flour mill owner named William Augustine Foote, who began tinkering with electricity not long after Thomas Alva Edison partnered with J.P. Morgan and a few wealthy New Yorkers in the early 1880s to bring light to their posh residences by powering his new light bulbs with small generators.

Foote imagined bringing Edison's electric light to the homes and streets of Michigan, but it wasn't until he and his engineering prodigy brother, J.B., teamed up with ironworks owner Samuel Jarvis that the dream came to incandescent life. Together, Foote and Jarvis created a company that has since been admired for its technical achievements, praised for its integrity, respected for its perseverance during challenging times and celebrated for its determination to make things better every day.

Consumers Energy's headquarters in Jackson, Mich., stands as a symbol of the company's commitment to customers and to Michigan. Consumers Energy restored a historic post office to its former glory as the grand entrance to a modern office tower. The building earned state and national awards for design, construction, historic preservation and environmental stewardship.

Trowbridge Dam, the birthplace of long-distance electrical transmission in Michigan, no longer generates electricity, but Consumers Energy has 13 other hydroelectric plants in operation that have been bringing power to the people and businesses of Michigan since the early 1900s.

2: "The

Lights Is Workin'!"

The vision and ingenuity of brothers J.B., standing, and W.A. Foote transformed life in Michigan for generations. This portrait hangs prominently in the restored Jackson Post Office section of the company's headquarters at One Energy Plaza.

Two very nervous men paced the banks of the Kalamazoo River near the village of Trowbridge, Mich., on Sept. 20, 1899, an unusually cool day for early autumn in these parts. A vision three years in the making and months of backbreaking work by crews of laborers and teams of horses was on the line, and things weren't happening as quickly as planned.

Over the previous year, tons of soil had been dug from the riverbanks and carefully deposited in huge, horse-drawn scoops into the swiftly moving river. A massive earthen dam arose, holding back a pond of water 22 feet deep. Below the dam, at the bottom of an 80-foot spillway, sat a 2,000-horsepower turbine propeller, ready for the water to start flowing and kick on a General Electric generator. It in turn would produce 2,500 volts of electricity.

About 25 miles away—at the other end of a rickety network of cheap iron wire strung on wooden poles 20 feet high—lay downtown Kalamazoo. There, another anxious man and an excited community of 17,000 people waited for the lights to come on by electricity for the very first time.

By the late 1890s, generating electricity by hydropower was becoming commonplace, though the effort to build the dams required was still herculean. The first hydroelectric dams had been constructed in Michigan 20 years earlier, but their direct-current (DC) power could only be put to use within a short distance of where it was produced—such as in Grand Rapids, where in 1880 a water turbine-powered dynamo lit a nearby opera house and a storefront.

As George Stecker and William Augustine ("W.A.") Foote stood by the Kalamazoo River that day in 1899, they were desperately hoping for a breakthrough that would help solve one of the thorniest challenges of the early days of electricity: generating power in one location and using it somewhere else. Stecker and Foote's younger brother, James Berry ("J.B.")

Foote—both self-taught engineers—had devised ingenious solutions to this problem for the Kalamazoo project, built on new generator technology using alternating-current (AC) power, which could travel much longer distances than DC.

Their inventions included a device that could regulate the flow of electric current so it remained steady even as demand on the line fluctuated, and they found a way to switch high-voltage electricity from one line to another in the event of a problem such as a short circuit.

Everything was to come together at this moment, when the turbine, the generator, the switches and a transformer that boosted the generator's 2,500 volts to an unheard-of 22,000 volts would be put to the test—and when

the world would find out whether a makeshift transmission system could reliably carry that much juice 25 miles by wire. As Stecker and W.A. Foote prepared to open the gate that would release the torrent, J.B. stood at the corner of Water and Edwards streets in Kalamazoo, watching for the lights to blink on.

W.A., a former miller who a decade earlier had decided that his future lay in bringing electricity to Michigan cities and towns, wasn't a demonstrative man. When the time came to set the works in motion, he nodded to the man who ran the powerhouse and said, simply, "Okay." The gates opened. Water poured forth. The generator rumbled to life. Lights crackled and illuminated the powerhouse. And then—nothing.

In the undeveloped countryside of

The Jackson Electric Light Works' first offices opened in 1888 in a two-story building off Mechanic Street. Below, an early company office.

The first street lighting in Adrian was powered by the arc-light generator in W.A. Foote's mill.

southwestern Michigan, long-distance telephone lines were rare. So W.A. and Stecker worried, pacing and waiting for word to arrive by less modern means. An hour went by. Then two. By the time nearly three hours had passed, the men had begun to lose faith.

Suddenly, clouds of dust along the road from Kalamazoo announced the arrival of a man on horseback. He reined in his horse on the river's west bank and called out breathlessly, "It's workin'!" He waved his sweat-drenched hat in triumph. "The lights is workin'!"

FINDING HIS DESTINY

W.A. Foote had only an eighth-grade education and very little money, but he had more determination than many men with advanced degrees and big bankrolls.

"He had to quit school to go to work to help support his family," great-great-granddaughter Lisa Carmoney told the *Jackson Citizen Patriot*

in 2011. "But everywhere he went, he had a science journal rolled up in his back pocket that he would pull out and read."

By 1884, Foote's ambition had landed the 30-year-old in nothing but a morass of debt. The flour mill he had opened in his hometown of Adrian, Mich., with borrowed funds was failing, and he was in desperate need of extra income. In a happy confluence of mutual need, men from the Massachusetts-based Thomson-Houston Electric Company, a manufacturing firm that was a precursor to General Electric, came calling. They were in search of a source of power for new streetlights they were installing in town, and the water power from Foote's mill would serve nicely. Foote was willing to take money wherever he could get it.

Thomson-Houston placed a generator inside the mill, and, as it turned out, it lit up more than Adrian's 12 arc-lamp streetlights: it ignited a new sense of purpose in W.A. As he listened to the generator's hum, Foote dreamed of a web of electric power that would someday replace the flickering of gas lamps with the steady glow of electric light on the streets, in homes and businesses and on farms throughout Michigan.

Foote decided he would no longer be a miller: his destiny lay in electricity. He signed his mill over to the businessman who'd financed it, borrowed money from another man and built a small electric plant with a Thomson-Houston generator to serve the 8,000 citizens of Adrian. One of W.A.'s first brilliant moves was to recruit his brother J.B., then just 17, as bookkeeper. Instinctively an engineer, J.B. had the ability to invent, build and make work almost anything that W.A.—visionary, salesman, money-raiser, businessman, entrepreneur—could dream up. Before long, J.B. was the company's chief engineer.

A lack of ambition was never W.A.'s problem, and no sooner was the Adrian plant operational than he had his eye on bigger things. He sold the plant and moved, with his brother, to Jackson. There, he partnered with Samuel Jarvis, the foreman of an iron and engine works in Lansing, who promised he could build the high-speed generators that Foote believed he would need to provide power for larger populations.

Jackson, a community with just under 20,000 people and, to Foote, unimpressive competition in the electricity business, would be his first target. In 1886, he approached the Jackson Common Council and made his case for "modern" electric streetlights. At the time, two companies—the Jackson Electric Light and Power Company and the Mitchell-Reid Company—had been valiantly trying to supply incandescent lighting to Jackson, with minimal success; most of downtown was still lit with gas lamps.

Foote proposed arc lighting, which used an electric current passed between two carbon electrodes, creating an arc. Light came from both the glow of the arc and the incandescence of the electrodes as they burned in open air. Six years earlier, in the summer of 1880, an entrepreneur and tinkerer named William Powers had illuminated parts of downtown Grand Rapids with arc lighting powered by a hydroelectric plant on the banks of the Grand River. The facility is widely regarded as the first hydroelectric plant in the United States.

Why, Foote exhorted the common council, should Jackson lag behind Grand Rapids

Arc lamps like this one over the Hotel Lawrence, above, illuminated Jackson's downtown in the 1890s and brought more customers to local businesses like the Martin & Giddings drugstore, below.

and other cities that had followed its lead? "Gentlemen, I ask your permission to erect poles, stretch wires and place a few electric streetlights on downtown thoroughfares," he implored. "I am not, at this point, asking for a franchise, only for permission to demonstrate the superiority of my arc lights."

The council consented, and soon workmen were busy on Main Street (today's Michigan Avenue) installing six "dishpan" lights, which used tin plates to reflect the arc lights' glow down toward the street. On Dec. 6, 1886, W.A.

Foote flipped a switch, and an assembled crowd uttered a collective gasp as an entire block of storefronts burst into glorious light. The Common Council granted Foote and Jarvis' Jackson Electric Light Works the franchise Foote had told them he was not yet asking for, and the company that would ultimately become Consumers Energy was on its way.

Within the next year, the Footes (who bought out Jarvis in the early 1900s) were able to raise enough funds to launch or acquire small electric companies in the neighboring towns of Battle

By the late 1890s, generating electricity by hydropower was becoming commonplace, though the effort to build the dams required was still herculean.

Creek, Albion and Kalamazoo. Those successes only meant, however, that the brothers needed more money to deliver on their promises to customers. Many things have changed about the utility business in the 130 years since arc lights first lit downtown Jackson, but one truth remains: major investments must be made in infrastructure and resources, often at great risk, long before any return on those investments can be expected.

For the next several years, W.A. and J.B. Foote and their families lived "on tea and potato peelings," as neighbors recounted in *Future Builders*, a history of Consumers Energy published in 1973. Engineer George Stecker, who'd been hired as the Footes' first employee before he received his high school diploma in 1889, received $25 per month to work 12-hour days, seven days a week—and often went without even that meager pay. He and many other employees were sometimes paid on Friday only to have their boss borrow the money back on Monday.

PUTTING IT TOGETHER

Riding the success of the Trowbridge project, Foote pursued additional hydroelectric ventures along the Kalamazoo River—the Otsego Dam and Plainwell Dams #1 and #2—and these formed the foundation of a network of high-voltage sources of power for distant communities. What distinguished W.A. Foote's vision in electricity's early days was that, where many saw a future in which dedicated power plants served prescribed communities with power produced specifically for them, Foote envisioned an interconnected system of generating stations, cities and towns throughout Michigan—where the power his many plants produced could be routed anywhere on the network based on demand and available supply. If he and J.B. were to achieve that vision, they'd need to expand their reach, consolidate their foothold, establish a critical mass and form partnerships.

A real estate developer from Muskegon named George Erwin, who had big dreams of building dams on the Muskegon River but little

When Croton went into operation in July 1908, transmitting 100,000 volts to Grand Rapids, word of its success spread around the world, and engineers from countries such as Russia, France and England traveled to see it.

V.G.Fargo – John W. Weadock – WM Eaton – E.F. Loud – Col George Loud – A.H Van Cleve – H.V. Schre..
...for Deck...

"Steerage"
Solomo...
Paddy MC...
George Im...
Wm (Billy)...
Al. Canit...

Ed Loud, J.C. Weadock, William Fargo and crew explored the Au Sable River for potential hydroelectric dam sites aboard a wanigan, a primitive, flat-bottomed version of a houseboat that could be disassembled and carried upstream by horse and wagon, then reassembled and floated downriver as investors scouted promising locations. Loud, whose lumber-baron family owned much of the land on either side of the Au Sable, had a fleet of three wanigans, named *Habitant, Voyageur* and *Dormant*, in honor of the region's French heritage.

practical notion of exactly how to do it, had bought up land rights along that river, pulling in fellow businessmen for money as he ran short. Erwin and his partners in the Grand Rapids-Muskegon Water Power Electric Company—which at that point was nothing more than an ambitious name—tried to hire away J.B. Foote to build dams for them, offering the Footes royalties in return.

"My brother works for nobody but me," W.A. responded firmly, whereupon he offered to buy out half of Erwin's interest in the company and build the dams for him. Eventually, Foote and Erwin agreed that, for a one-third share of the Grand Rapids-Muskegon company, Foote would be a silent partner in the venture.

By 1904, Foote had a burgeoning empire of utility companies and generating facilities. He merged them all that year into a single company, Commonwealth Power, headquartered in Jackson, by now the home of 238 luminous-arc lamps. It was really an empire in name only, though, as it served just 2,472 households

and businesses, many of which were actually customers of the gas companies Foote had acquired in the early 1900s.

"THIS HAS NEVER BEEN DONE BEFORE"

In 1904, Foote commissioned three new dams: Rogers and Croton on the Muskegon, and Webber on the Grand River. The Rogers Dam was finished first, in early 1906. Its generators spat out 7,200 volts of electricity that reached 72,000 volts—the highest voltage anywhere in the world at the time—after coursing through three transformers.

A year later, Foote outdid Rogers with the grand opening of the Croton Dam, 16 miles downriver on the Muskegon. Built with a new construction method called hydraulic sluicing, which was well suited for earth embankment dams on soft soils, Croton housed two turbine-driven generators rated at 6,600 volts. When the Croton transmission line to Grand Rapids went live in July 1908—at 100,000 volts, then the highest-voltage line in the world—word spread rapidly. Engineers from as far away as Russia, Japan and India traveled weeks by ship, train and wagon to reach what were still the wilds of western Michigan to see the facility. Dr. Charles Steinmetz, the German mathematician and electrical engineer who had helped give birth to the U.S. electric power industry with his revolutionary work on alternating current, traveled from his laboratory at General Electric in Schenectady, N.Y., to conduct tests on the lines from Croton. Awestruck, he told his companions, "To think, gentlemen, that this has never been done before."

The Footes built to last. The Rogers and Croton dams are still in operation today, generating more than 15,000 kilowatts of electricity. Consumers Power built yet another dam on the Muskegon River, the much larger Hardy Dam, as part of its last hydro project in 1931. Together, the three Muskegon River facilities can generate about 45,500 kilowatts and serve a community of nearly 23,000 people.

CONSOLIDATING POWER

W.A. Foote was not the only savvy businessman making waves in Michigan's utility industry at the turn of the 20th century. As Commonwealth Power was on its way to controlling most of the electric utilities in western Michigan, a partnership between a banker from Grand Rapids and a gas man from Kalamazoo was doing a similar thing on the eastern side of the state—and beyond.

Operating out of an office in the financial center of New York, Anton G. Hodenpyl, who had been born in Grand Rapids and founded the Michigan Trust Company, and Kalamazoo-born Henry D. Walbridge, president of Grand Rapids Gas Light Company, had been buying up gas and electric utilities as well as trolley lines throughout the Midwest and East. By the time Foote formed Commonwealth Power in 1904, the deeper-pocketed Hodenpyl-Walbridge & Company had interests in New York, Pennsylvania, Illinois and Indiana, and their Michigan Light Company controlled most of the gas and electric utilities in eastern Michigan outside of Detroit—notably in Pontiac and Saginaw. They also owned gas businesses that competed with Commonwealth's electricity operations in Jackson and Kalamazoo.

It was inevitable that these two determined forces would meet, and that they would either clash or combine. The latter came to pass

In 1904, the Footes consolidated their power companies under the name Commonwealth Power Co., seen on the 1910-era field car, below. The Footes had begun by lighting busy streets in Jackson and Adrian, but by the early part of the 20th century, they also served residential neighborhoods in Grand Rapids, above.

TRANSFORM
CORE.
140,000 V.
Zilwaukee,
Mich
1911.

beginning in 1908, as the two competitors wooed a lumberman named Edward Loud, each hoping to acquire land that Loud—with his own dreams of building hydroelectric dams—had purchased up and down the banks of the Au Sable River. An extraordinary turn of events took place that summer in which W.A. Foote met with Loud and the Hodenpyl-Walbridge team, and discussions produced an understanding that Commonwealth and Hodenpyl-Walbridge would put their interests together. It took two years to work out the details, but at last, in 1910, the companies merged, incorporating as Consumers Power Company, with W.A. Foote as president, under a holding company called Commonwealth Power Railway & Light Company.

The merger set off a frenzy of construction along the Au Sable. Consumers Power built three dams—Cooke, Five Channels and Loud—within three years. Ultimately, there were six, including Foote, Mio and Alcona, the last completed in 1924 after a delay caused by World War I.

At last, W.A.'s vision of an interconnected system transmitting power throughout Michigan could be fulfilled—but only if Consumers Power could find someone to make the complex switches and connections function. In those days, coordinating electrical services was an unknown endeavor even to most people in the power business, J.B. Foote included. But the company was able to find one man, 30-year-old Timothy A. Kenney, with the right experience. Kenney had been assistant operating manager at New York's Hudson River Power Transmission Company, one of the few electric companies in the country that had even a modest central switching operation.

Kenney and J.B. Foote built a dispatching nerve center at Consumers Power's Trail Street steam plant in Jackson. It directed voltage and frequency, switched communities between lines as demand required, and powered generators on and off at a moment's notice. What the pair built was nothing less than the grandfather of modern electrical distribution—and a system that, at its core, was not all that different from the central dispatching center that Consumers Energy operates today on Parnall Road, north of Jackson, to handle the demands of 1.8 million customers.

W.A. Foote lived to see the dispatching center open, but he would not witness the 1918 completion of the hydroelectric dam that would one day bear his name. As he was about to leave for New York on the morning of April 12, 1915, Foote was stricken with a heart attack and died at the age of 60. His brother, plagued by kidney problems, carried on as the company leadership passed into another man's hands.

The kite and lightning bolt in Commonwealth's 1915 logo recalled Benjamin Franklin's experiments with electricity, while the key symbolized a future to be unlocked with electric power. As voltage on transmission lines increased in the early 1910s, insulator testing trucks such as the one below were essential. The 140,000-volt Zilwaukee transmission line dwarfed the capacity of earlier lines, and its transformer core, opposite, even dwarfed its technicians.

In 1927, the company opened a general office on West Michigan Avenue. It replaced a makeshift aggregation of buildings that afforded employees little comfort or privacy. Consumers Power would occupy this imposing, 11-story building for the next 76 years.

THE GREAT WAR AND BEYOND

After W.A. Foote's death, Henry Walbridge's protégé, Bernard Capen Cobb, became president of both Commonwealth Power Railway & Light and Consumers Power, while Charles W. Tippy, an experienced gas man with Hodenpyl-Walbridge, applied his considerable intellect to the electric side of the business as Consumers Power's general manager. Walbridge and Hodenpyl parted ways around this time, and businessman George E. Hardy—who would ultimately give his name to Consumers Power's third dam on the Muskegon—became Hodenpyl's partner.

In June 1922, Consumers Power and Michigan Light Company, the former Hodenpyl-Walbridge operation, merged into a single entity, bringing all of the company's Michigan gas and electric properties together. With this, the pace of growth accelerated, and Consumers Power added more sources of energy and connected ever more customers to its expanding grid. Within a few years, Consumers

Power had snapped up other utilities in the state: Thornapple Gas and Electric, Southern Michigan Light and Power, Lansing Fuel and Gas, Charlotte Gas Company and Citizens Electric Company.

Consumers Power opened its first coal-fired generation facility, the 80,000-kilowatt Saginaw River steam generating plant, in 1924. Two years later, a deceptively simple invention—a natural gas-powered water heater designed by Consumers Power gas operations chief James A. Brown and his colleague William Handley Sr.—gave households access to gas-heated water around the clock. Sales of gas and the clever device itself went into overdrive.

Thanks to the Handley-Brown water heater, Consumers Power's roster of gas customers shot from a little more than 60,000 in 1921 to 162,590 in 1929; the number of electric customers also jumped, from around 130,000 to nearly 300,000 in the same period. With this growth came profit, and Consumers Power's earnings increased every year between 1922 and 1929. Very few low points punctuated these go-go years, but one of them took place in May 1924, when J.B. Foote—still the company's chief engineer after almost 40 years—succumbed to his kidney problems. He was just shy of his 57th birthday.

FROM BUBBLES TO PAY CUTS

By 1924, it had been nearly 30 years since George Stecker and W.A. Foote had heard those reassuring words from the rider from Kalamazoo—"The lights is workin'!" The lights were now on statewide in Michigan, but only in cities and towns. Rural areas remained largely cut off from electric power; a survey showed that less than 3 percent of the state's farms were electrified.

Charles Tippy was determined to convince skeptical farmers that electricity was the wave of the agricultural future. On Feb. 4, 1927, Consumers Power extended a transmission line seven miles to serve 33 farms between Mason and Dansville as a test project. It was the beginning of rural electrification in Michigan—indeed, in the United States—and farmers along the Mason-Dansville line were the first rural power users in the nation.

By that time, Consumers Power had outgrown its headquarters in Jackson. On July 13, 1927, Tippy struck a "champagne" bottle filled with water from the 13 Michigan rivers that powered Consumers Power's plants against the granite doorway of a new, 11-story office building on West Michigan Avenue in Jackson. This bubbly act of optimism was in many ways the exclamation point on an era of increased focus and extraordinary expansion that would soon come to an end.

The popularity of the automobile and the presence of new bus systems in large cities had put pressure on Commonwealth Power Railway

& Light's many passenger rail properties, and in 1924 Cobb had broken the holding company in two, creating Commonwealth Power Corporation for the company's electricity ventures and Electric Railway Securities Company, whose sole purpose was to liquidate the rail businesses. Four years later, Cobb presided over one of the largest acquisitions in company history when Commonwealth gained control of Southeastern Power & Light Company, which provided service in Mississippi, Alabama, Georgia and part of Florida.

A series of corporate reorganizations took place, Hodenpyl-Hardy went out of business, layers of new holding companies were created, and by the time the stock market

Consumers Power's Saginaw River steam generating plant at Zilwaukee, below, was built in 1924. It was expanded several times and became one of the company's largest steam plants before being taken out of service in 1972.

Consumers Power's experiment to extend an electric line between the farming communities of Mason and Dansville was so novel that the activation of the lines drew crowds. Farmers granted the company a right-of-way to string and service transmission towers, opposite.

crash of October 1929 lit the fuse on the Great Depression, Consumers Power was part of a vast network of 165 subsidiaries whose ultimate corporate parent was named The Commonwealth & Southern Corporation.

Initially, Cobb simultaneously held the presidencies of Commonwealth, Consumers Power and several other companies, but he resigned as Consumers Power's president in 1932 and was succeeded by Timothy Kenney, the man who had designed Consumers Power's innovative dispatching system. In January of the following year, Cobb, in ill health, left Commonwealth & Southern altogether. He was succeeded by a tall, shambling, tough-minded lawyer and former Army captain named Wendell Willkie, who would use his tenacious leadership of Commonwealth as the springboard to a political career.

In the meantime, the Depression had hit industrial states such as Michigan particularly hard. By 1933, Michigan's economic engine, the auto industry, had slowed production by 60 percent. Half of all the industrial workers in the state were out of a job. Consumers Power's gross revenues dropped by 22 percent, and all employees and officers took a 10 percent pay cut—with the exception of general manager

Tippy, who silently cut his pay by 20 percent.

Willkie's planned path out of the Depression was to aggressively promote the use of electric power and boost consumption. He led the company to test and refine electric appliances such as refrigerators, stoves and water heaters in its own laboratory, and to sell them to consumers.

Beginning in 1933, in part because of Willkie's deft marketing ideas and in part because of an improving economy, Consumers Power's revenues and earnings were growing again. Revenues were back to 1929 levels by 1936, although it would be some time before earnings caught up with that growth.

BENEATH THE EARTH

It's a truism of the utility business that investments in tomorrow's energy innovations must be made today, even if today the wolf is at the door. So it was that in 1931, Consumers Power had taken a headlong dive into the natural gas distribution business, recognizing that gas was more efficient than electricity for some uses, such as heating, and that customers would want choice in energy sources well into the future.

A moderately sized natural gas field was discovered in 1931 in Broomfield Township, about 45 miles west of Bay City in central Michigan. Consumers Power began buying gas from Broomfield, and the company laid a 40-mile pipeline between the wellheads and the town of Midland to carry it east. Consumers Power determined that the Michigan bedrock contained enough natural gas to supply customers in its Bay City and Saginaw territories, where the company had been buying coal from outside suppliers to manufacture gas in a costly and dirty process. Replacing that manufactured gas with natural gas piped in from Broomfield could reduce prices by as much as 79 percent, lowering costs to Consumers Power and therefore to its customers.

Michigan's natural gas reserves weren't inexhaustible, though, and if Consumers Power truly wanted to succeed in this new business, it would need a large and steady supply of natural

Consumers Power's logo from 1949 showed a service territory that covered nearly the entire state of Michigan. Opposite, the statewide operation of an interconnected generation and transmission system was under the 24-hour direction of dispatchers in 1947.

gas. In the late 1930s, Daniel Karn, who had succeeded Tippy as Consumers Power's general manager, struck a deal to tap into the Michigan extension of the new Panhandle Eastern pipeline, which brought gas northeast from oil country: Texas, Oklahoma and Kansas. By 1941, Consumers Power had contracted to purchase up to 25 million cubic feet of natural gas per day from the pipeline, converting major cities such as Flint, Pontiac and Jackson, as well as the Detroit suburbs, from manufactured to natural gas.

Over the next two decades, the industrial demands of World War II revived Michigan from the ravages of the Depression, and a newly independent Consumers Power—which would separate from Commonwealth & Southern in 1949 following a prolonged battle over the requirements of 1935's Public Utility Holding Company Act (PUHCA), which broke up most utility holding companies—built five new generating plants. The first, J.C. Weadock, opened with fanfare in 1940, just in time to provide much of the electricity for Michigan's contribution to the war effort—mostly vehicles and weapons—and right before Wendell Willkie left Consumers Power for an unsuccessful presidential bid against President Franklin D. Roosevelt in 1940.

The war pushed Consumers Power to its limits. With the defense industry's plants running around the clock, there was barely enough power to go around. The company was forced to drive its generating units past their

rated capacities and postpone maintenance in order to keep assembly lines turning out the guns and Jeeps desperately needed overseas. As substation operators, women replaced the men who were off in the trenches. Meters were read only every second month. Construction screeched to a halt; an expansion of the new Weadock plant, for example, had to be put off until after the war.

After the Allies declared victory in 1945, the company opened four more fossil-fuel complexes to feed the state's postwar industrial boom: B.C. Cobb near Muskegon in 1949, J.R. Whiting at the head of Lake Erie in 1952, D.E. Karn on Saginaw Bay in 1959 and J.H. Campbell—which at 1,450 megawatts was the most powerful steam plant Consumers Power has ever operated—near Holland in 1962. These plants, all named for leaders who had helped to build the company, burned coal, natural gas or oil to heat water; the steam produced helped spin turbines to generate electricity. Together, they added more than 4,100 kilowatts of electricity to Consumers Power's system.

In the meantime, Consumers Power expanded its natural gas business far beyond what the cautious Daniel Karn might have imagined when he inked that first tentative deal with Panhandle. Another pipeline, the Trunkline-Consumers Power system, completed in the spring of 1960, brought large reserves of gas from the Gulf Coast. In 1963, at a sealed-bid price of $20 million, Consumers Power acquired the production properties and exploration leases

of Panhandle Eastern in Michigan—a deal that grew the company's book of business, even if only in theory for the moment, to include not only gas transmission and distribution, but production as well.

Consumers Power created a subsidiary called Northern Michigan Exploration Company (NOMECO) to pursue gas exploration and production. Initial exploration in Michigan's Lower Peninsula yielded only dry wells, and the company turned its attention elsewhere. After several years, having invested $40 million to explore in southern Louisiana, NOMECO struck metaphorical gold as one well after another, onshore and off, hit gas. Then, in northern Michigan, at previously unplumbed depths of 7,000 feet below the surface, NOMECO discovered billions of cubic feet of natural gas reserves.

Still, all this new energy would not be enough to meet the unprecedented postwar demands of Michigan's homes, farms and businesses. For that, Consumers Power, like many American utilities at the time, turned to a technology best known for its destructive power and its association with the Japanese cities of Hiroshima and Nagasaki: nuclear fission.

GOING NUCLEAR
President Dwight D. Eisenhower signed the Atomic Energy Act in 1954, providing for the private use and development of nuclear power for peaceful means. That was the same year in which a nuclear plant in Russia first generated

This traveling kitchen of the 1950s was the brainchild of appliance sales supervisor Howard Davis, who sought a solution to the challenge of getting more rural customers into the company's showrooms. In 1935, Davis ordered the first of a series of large streamliners from the Aero-Car Sales Corporation, featuring a sparkling white kitchen that could show off a dazzling array of major appliances.

electricity for a power grid and in which Lewis Strauss, chairman of the U.S. Atomic Energy Commission, suggested that nuclear plants could generate electricity at a cost "too cheap to meter."

It was also the year that an energetic senior vice president of Consumers Power named James H. "Jim" Campbell led the company into a coalition of two dozen organizations interested in learning about nuclear power and whether it might be effective, especially in producing baseload for utilities.

In 1958, Campbell attended a high-level meeting on nuclear power organized by General Electric in California and came back convinced that nuclear generation was the way of the future. He was so fired up, in fact, that the first

thing he did on returning was to walk into the office of his executive assistant, Robert Allen, and say, "Bob, how would you like to get into the nuclear business?"

With the backing of Daniel Karn, by then Consumers Power's president, and over the objection of some skeptics, Campbell pushed the company into the nuclear age. Before a year had passed, Consumers Power signed contracts to build a $25 million nuclear plant near Charlevoix on Lake Michigan. Named Big Rock Point after a large nearby boulder that was once a landmark for Odawa Native Americans, the plant opened in 1962 as the fifth commercial nuclear power plant in the United States and the world's first high-power density boiling-water reactor. Its maximum output was 75,000 kilowatts–a

To spur demand for electricity and natural gas, Consumers Power sold appliances—as well as the energy that powered them—as a key part of its strategy into the 1950s. This mid-20th century advertisement is one in a series the company produced to show how idyllic home life could be thanks to the conveniences of modern electric appliances.

Powered by Natural Gas

The expansion of Consumers Power's gas business and infrastructure powered much of the company's prosperity through the 1950s and 1960s. Indeed, as a gas company alone, Consumers Power would have ranked among the top 10 natural gas utilities in the country.

By the 1990s, however, the company's gas business was getting little attention and had become undervalued. In 1995, to give the gas operation more prominence and take advantage of new growth opportunities, Consumers Power created separate strategic business units (SBUs) for gas and electric.

"We were so serious about this that CMS Energy put a separate tracking stock—the 'G' stock—on the New York Stock Exchange," says Terence Mierzwa, now chief of staff in the CEO's office who at the time was director of marketing for the gas business. "That allowed investors to more directly invest in our gas business."

Dave Joos—who was so frugal with electricity use at home that his young son once volunteered to pay him three cents a night to keep his night light on—was named head of the electric SBU. Paul Elbert led the gas SBU and was given the mandate of turning it into a significant growth engine.

The effort included the traditional approach of knocking on doors to recruit more gas customers.

"Michigan had a lot of households using

In the 1920s, Consumers Power and Detroit City Gas reached an agreement to divide the natural gas service territory north of Detroit. As crews laid pipes throughout Oakland County, below, the area grew to become the company's single most lucrative territory for residential gas sales, providing more than one-third of the company's gas income by the early 1970s.

The 24-mile Southwest Michigan Pipeline, shown above under construction near Coldwater, began operation in September 2014. It completed a 90-mile, dual gas pipeline that allows Consumers Energy to safely and reliably transport large volumes of natural gas to customers.

propane at the time," Mierzwa recalls. "It was an easy fix on your furnace or water heater to change over to natural gas. We also had a lot of farms with big grain dryers operating on propane, which we switched to natural gas."

To go "beyond the meter" in expanding the company's natural gas business, Mierzwa and his team developed value-added products and services, the first of which was a then-novel Appliance Service Plan (ASP).

"We had a commitment to respond to gas leak reports in less than 30 minutes, and we needed a labor force capacity to meet that—which meant that we sometimes had excess labor. The original idea was, hey, let's send them out to fix furnaces." Soon, Consumers Power extended its program of repairing furnaces for a fee to gas water heaters, ranges and dryers, and expanded it from the Detroit metropolitan area to the gas system statewide. Later, the company began servicing electric appliances. Today, the ASP program serves more than 200,000 customers and brings in more than $70 million in annual revenue.

In 1999, Carl English assumed leadership of the gas SBU when Paul Elbert took a post

in Chicago. A 30-year company veteran, English combined a deep sense of "servant leadership"—putting others above himself—with a wicked penchant for practical jokes that included filling the media relations director's file cabinet with limburger cheese.

English's mischievous humor belied a tireless work ethic. He frequently arrived at work at 4 a.m. to answer emails and get a jump on the day.

"We want to be the utility that customers value," he said. "At heart, it's really as simple as that. To be a strong natural gas utility that's able to seize and capitalize on opportunities for future growth. We need to continue to do an excellent job in the utility, in both distribution and service, because it's the foundation from which everything else springs."

When English took a new position in Ohio in 2004, John Russell, already president of Consumers Energy's electric division, assumed English's post as president of the gas division as well. The gas and electric SBUs were reintegrated three years later—the combined effects of volatile commodity prices and declining gas prices in a laggard economy rendering the SBU structure no longer efficient. But after a dozen years as a separate unit, Consumers Energy's natural gas business had re-established its importance. Indeed, the company's 1997 name change from Consumers Power to Consumers Energy was made in part to stress the company's comprehensive book of business.

Today, as Michigan's largest gas utility, Consumers possesses the infrastructure and expertise to safely distribute natural gas to 1.7 million customers in 45 counties. The company is investing hundreds of millions of dollars to upgrade its infrastructure. Projects include a new, 24-mile natural gas pipeline in Southwest Michigan and a $500 million effort to inspect, assess and replace its existing pipeline system. The company also is increasing its use of natural gas as a cheaper, cleaner fuel source to generate electricity as Michigan shifts away from coal.

A wide-angle view of construction of the Big Rock Point nuclear plant shows the iconic spherical containment structure, above. Operators in the control room, right, were focused and intense as the world's first boiling water direct-cycle, forced circulation, high-power density nuclear reactor facility went critical on Sept. 27, 1962. Visitors to the plant were welcomed by a film, "Headstart on Tomorrow," narrated by a young Ronald Reagan, opposite.

relative baby by today's standards—but it proved that Consumers Power could get the job done, and it taught the company how to successfully harness the atom to generate power.

The success of Big Rock Point proved Campbell's case for nuclear energy, and in 1966—by which time he had become Consumers Power's president—Campbell doubled down on the nuclear bet. The company announced plans to build a $100 million, 200-megawatt plant five miles south of South Haven on the Lake Michigan shore. The Palisades Nuclear Plant would be what then-Consumers Power Senior Vice President Russell Youngdahl referred to as "one of the big boys" among nuclear facilities. Local news media exulted that a fairy godmother had come to Van Buren County.

That's not exactly what came to pass.

A baby born in 1967, the year the Midland Nuclear Plant began construction, would have been nearly eligible to vote by the time Consumers Energy abandoned the controversial project in 1984. Consumers Energy ultimately turned Midland into a successful cogeneration facility— and a symbol of the company's own repeated rises from near ashes.

3: Building Boom

The decades between the end of World War II and the beginning of the 1970s were in many ways a golden age of energy, the forces of extraordinary demand, increasing capacity, higher efficiency and excellent profits coming together to allow Consumers Power to provide customers with a seemingly limitless amount of power and ever better service at ever lower rates.

Between 1948 and 1969, Consumers Power constructed 14 fossil-fueled generating units at its Campbell, Weadock, Karn, Cobb and Whiting plants, which in sum produced 4,100 megawatts of electricity for Michigan's booming economy. On a kilowatt-hour basis, average prices for residential power declined from the equivalent of $4 in 1892 to 9 cents in 1967.

"The utility people wore the white hats," recalls Ted Vogel, who came to Consumers Power as a young lawyer in the 1970s and stayed for 36 years, rising to vice president and chief tax counsel. "In the 1950s and 1960s, everything was constantly getting bigger and better, and usage was growing by 4 to 5 percent every year." As a result, Vogel said, Consumers Power could lower rates while remaining profitable enough to invest in the system's reliability and growth and take care of shareholders.

As the 1960s neared an end, it appeared abundant and inexpensive energy would last forever, with new plants coming online and the company enjoying a casual and cordial relationship with the Michigan Public Service Commission (MPSC). Consumers Power, its customers and its shareholders all reaped the benefits.

"THE PROJECT" ON THE BLUFF
The construction boom continued into the 1970s, and the first new plant to open that decade was the Ludington Pumped Storage Facility on the Lake Michigan shore. A team of Consumers Power engineers had developed the

Consumers Power's fossil-fuel fleet grew dramatically between the 1940s and 1970s. The B.C. Cobb plant, whose 1949 dedication is pictured above, encompassed five coal-fueled units by 1957. Opposite, workers build a discharge duct at the J.C. Weadock plant in Hampton Township on June 4, 1948.

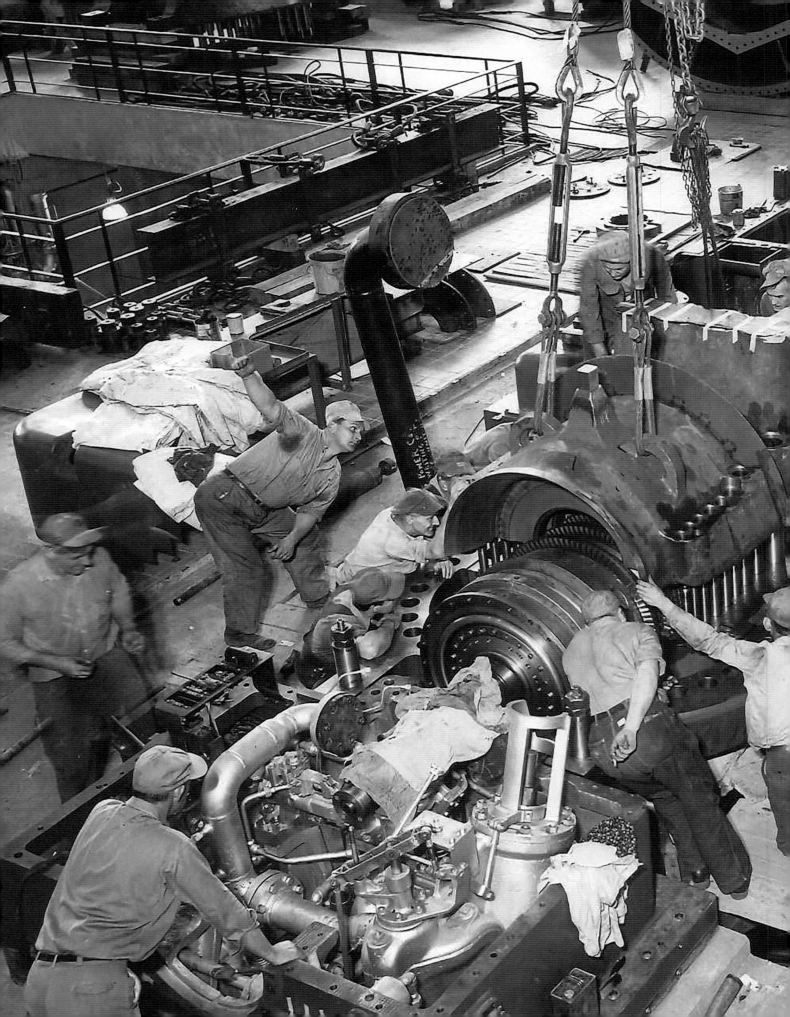

Workers assemble Turbine 3 for the last of the J.R. Whiting Generating Complex's three units on Sept. 11, 1953. One of the smallest coal-fired plants in the company's portfolio, Whiting began producing energy in 1952. Pressure from water boiling to steam would turn the turbine's fan blades at 3,600 revolutions per minute. Below, a Consumers Power promotional piece from 1954.

Serving Outstate Michigan with Electricity and Gas

CONSUMERS

Seen from the bluff above it, below, and across the lake, opposite, the Ludington Pumped Storage Facility begins to emerge from the Lake Michigan shoreline in the early 1970s. The reservoir, 2.5 miles long and one mile wide, has not yet begun to take shape in these photos. Building a plant such as Ludington today would likely cost more than $1 billion, according to former plant manager Bill Schoenlein.

concept in the 1950s as a way for the utility to respond to spikes in demand without purchasing power from outside suppliers on the expensive spot market. The idea gained traction after a series of power outages in the 1960s and a resulting power-sharing agreement between Consumers Power and Detroit Edison.

A hydroelectric facility combining a reservoir that holds as much water as 2 million backyard swimming pools, six 1,100-foot-long penstocks and six powerful turbines, Ludington was designed to be able to produce electricity minutes after being switched on. At maximum output, it could power a city of 1.4 million people.

Consumers Power investigated more than 60 possible locations for the plant. It chose the harbor town of Ludington because of the unique landscape featuring the bluff south of town near the Pere Marquette River, and its proximity to nearby port facilities and to cities where energy

use was high, such as Grand Rapids and Lansing. Construction began in 1969.

Locals, who dubbed the facility "the project," flocked to the site during four years of construction, watching in fascination as the 1,000-acre facility took shape. As large as it was, the plant—in which water from a huge reservoir would drop more than 300 feet under high pressure to turn six powerful turbines and produce electricity—harmonized with the surrounding landscape so well that travelers driving by on nearby roads often didn't know it was there.

"The project," which ultimately cost $327 million, proved to be a major economic driver for the community, as the town overflowed with engineers, electricians, welders and other workers, and many local asphalt and aggregate businesses still in operation today got their start building the plant. At the peak of construction,

more than 2,800 people worked there. They moved more than 50 million cubic yards of earth, stabilized the embankment's outer slope with 37,000 pounds of grass seed, coated the dikes of the upper reservoir with 500,000 tons of asphalt concrete liner, and installed and connected all the hydraulic and electric systems and electronic controls.

The last of Ludington's six turbines went into commercial operation in October 1973– within just 20 days of a schedule that had been established three years before construction began. At the time, Ludington was the largest facility of its kind in the world (it's the fifth-largest today). It earned recognition from the American Society of Civil Engineers (ASCE) as the outstanding civil engineering achievement of 1973. The Michigan section of ASCE later named Ludington one of Michigan's Top 10 civil engineering projects for the 20th century.

MAN-MADE GAS

Manufactured gas made a reappearance in Michigan in the 1970s–if only briefly. It had been rendered all but obsolete by the network of natural gas pipelines that, beginning in the 1930s, carried fuel from hydrocarbon fields in the West and South to markets north and east. But fluctuations in natural gas supplies drove Consumers Power's purchase costs higher while caps on the prices the utility could charge customers made distributing natural gas an unacceptably low-margin–and often money-losing–proposition.

John Simpson, then Consumers Power's senior vice president of gas operations, believed the company needed to diversify the sources of gas for its customers. Thus on the cloudy morning of July 8, 1971, Simpson climbed into the cab of a backhoe in a forest clearing near Marysville, Mich., to ceremonially break ground

Still Running After 100 Years

W.A. and J.B. Foote would probably find much about the Consumers Energy of today strange and wondrous—the solar arrays, wind farms, the Ludington Pumped Storage Facility, the 27,000 miles of company transmission lines and gas pipelines that cross the Michigan landscape. Some things they'd recognize right away, though: walking along the banks of rivers like the Muskegon, Au Sable or Grand, they'd see many of the hydroelectric plants they built—Cooke, Croton, Five Channels, Loud, Mio, Rogers, Webber—still operating 100 years later.

"They really did a great job of building these things," says Don Baker, supervisor of hydro operations for Consumers Energy.

Consumers Energy's 13 hydroelectric plants on five Michigan rivers have a combined generating capacity of about 130 megawatts, and they produce roughly 450,000 megawatt-hours of electricity per year, enough to serve 70,000 people. Although their contribution to Consumers Energy's total generating capacity is small at about 2 percent per year, the hydros are an important part of the company's legacy and history. The founders learned their craft, pushed technical boundaries, built their business and established the company's reputation by taming rugged landscapes and unstable, gravelly soils, harnessing rushing water to produce electricity, and delivering it longer and longer distances to people who needed it.

Croton, located on the Muskegon River, was one of three hydro plants the Footes commissioned in 1904, and it was considered

With a capacity of 3,225 kilowatts, the Webber dam and hydroelectric plant began generating electricity in 1907. The 32-foot high, 1,200-foot long dam is the tallest on the Grand River. Behind it lies a seven-mile long, 660-acre reservoir.

Five Channels Dam, below, completed in 1912, was the second of six hydroelectric dams built by Consumers Power on the Au Sable River. During construction, the company developed a 45-acre camp for workers and their families, complete with a central water supply and sewage system, icehouse, school, washroom, store and boardinghouse. As part of their compensation, workers also received land on which to build a house.

among the greatest engineering achievements in Michigan history at the time for the ingenuity of its method of construction, for its power and for the ability of its transmission line to carry an unprecedented load of 100,000 volts. Croton is one of only 20 facilities in the United States that, because of technical achievements or longevity, have been inducted into the Hydro Hall of Fame by *Hydro Review* magazine.

When Consumers Energy celebrated Croton's centennial in 2007, it opened the plant's doors to the public for the first time. More than 1,000 people stood in line for as long as an hour for a tour. A vintage baseball game, played by 1907 rules and without mitts, was recreated between the Ludington Mariners and the Coopersville Muldoons of Grand Rapids, professional minor-league teams from the early 1900s, and a historical walking tour led visitors to the home of Alfred Wyss, Croton's first and longest-serving plant operator. The Swiss-born Wyss retired in 1944 after 44 years of continuous service to the company at Croton, the Tippy Dam on the Manistee River and several other hydro facilities.

The hydros were able to withstand the torrential rains of September 1986, which caused 100-year flooding across about 14,000 square miles of Michigan, from north of Muskegon, east across all of central Lower Michigan and into the state's Thumb. Rivers

throughout Michigan, including the Muskegon, on which Consumers Energy operates three hydro plants, reached record crest levels. Emergency crews worked extended overnight duty to keep Hardy, Croton and Rogers from overtopping, preventing an unimaginable amount of destruction downstream. As soon as the rain ended and sun broke through, Consumers Power repair crews—some rowing boats to navigate waist-deep water—got to work restoring electricity to the battered region and the company's relieved customers.

To this day, when maintaining or upgrading Consumers Energy's hydro plants, Baker and his staff work with original drawings that bear the names of Foote, engineer George Stecker and some of the company's other early designers. For example, in 2008, Consumers Energy needed to upgrade one of the turbines at the Hardy plant, designed in the 1920s by company engineer Edward Burd based on concepts pioneered by the Footes' consulting engineer, William Fargo, in the late 1800s. Hardy went into service in 1932.

"We had to upgrade the turbine runner and rebuild the generator, which yielded an efficiency gain of 6 percent," Baker says of the 2008 retrofit. "That says a lot about how good the original designs were—a hydroelectric plant built in 1932 is upgraded with modern technology, for a gain of just 6 percent. Really, for the last 40 years, we've just been maintaining and running them."

on the nation's first gas reforming plant.

Crude oil that comes straight out of the ground isn't very useful in its raw state. It must be refined into finished products of varying weights and purity. It can be "reformed" into gas in a complicated process that separates hydrocarbons from the oil into various liquids; purifies, vaporizes and heats the liquids; and then passes them over a catalyst. The result is a manufactured gas of essentially the same composition and combustion quality as natural gas.

The Marysville Gas Reforming Plant opened on September 27, 1973, tapping into a branch of Canada's Interprovincial-Lakehead pipeline for a feedstock of crude sufficient to produce 100 million cubic feet of gas per day. This was later boosted to 220 million cubic feet per day.

Less than two weeks after Marysville opened, the Yom Kippur War broke out in the Middle East, ultimately prompting an oil embargo against the United States. The embargo combined with declining domestic oil output to produce a long-lasting energy shock marked by fuel shortages and skyrocketing prices, long lines at gas stations and, eventually, a new dedication to conservation.

By 1977, gas and fuel oil shortages in the Midwest had reached crisis levels, and a severe cold snap rapidly drained natural gas supplies. Throughout the Midwest, states began to curtail industry, preserving supplies for hospitals, schools and homes. Gas-heated schools in Columbus, Ohio, closed for a month. Indiana utilities asked all gas-burning offices and stores in the northern third of the state to close temporarily.

The investment in Marysville meant that Michigan businesses and homes served by Consumers Power stayed open, safe and warm through an icy and seemingly endless winter. "At the peak of its use, Marysville was producing 25 percent of all the gas used by our customers," former Consumers Energy lawyer Ted Vogel says. "It essentially kept the state from shutting down."

Ultimately, however, synthetic gas would prove too costly to be a long-term solution for

The Marysville Gas Reforming Plant operated for just six years, from 1973 to 1979, but it helped keep the power on in Michigan during the energy crisis.

Making Life Better

Walt Gable wants to introduce you to the future — a future powered with abundant energy.

Walt is coordinator of nuclear information at our Palisades nuclear plant, 35 miles west of Kalamazoo. He shows visitors the world of the future — an expanding world in which electric power plays an ever greater role. ■ By 1975 we expect to generate 50 percent more electricity than today — at Palisades, at a new pumped storage hydroelectric plant near Ludington, and at a future nuclear plant near Midland. ■ Consumers Power is building today for Michigan's tomorrow. Because we care about making life better for all of us.

Consumers Power

General Offices: Jackson, Mich.

In the early 1970s, nuclear power was heralded as the clean energy of the future.

stability in gas supply or price, and Consumers Power had its own problems with cost overruns on construction at Marysville that generated consumer and regulatory backlash. The company shut the Marysville plant down in 1979.

THE NUCLEAR DRAMA

Consumers Power added to its fossil-plant portfolio with two new units at Karn in the mid-1970s and a third unit at Campbell that would open in 1980, but those efforts even combined with the projects at Ludington and Marysville were dwarfed by Consumers Power's major focus in the 1970s: nuclear power.

At the time Consumers Power announced the development of the Palisades Nuclear Plant in 1966, it was to be one of the largest nuclear generating facilities in the nation. As with so many nuclear projects of the era, getting Palisades built was no easy matter. Challenges from environmental groups delayed completion by almost a year, and Consumers Power had to install $15 million of pollution control equipment before the Atomic Energy Commission (AEC) would grant its license. By the time Palisades came online in December 1971–producing its first electricity on New Year's Eve–costs had ballooned from a projected $100 million to more than $188 million.

Despite these setbacks, all seemed well with Palisades at first. Like any nuclear plant, it was a high-pressure work environment, recalls Tom Elward, who joined Consumers Power in 1972 as a nuclear engineer to help with the plant's startup.

"Professionalism and standards on the nuclear side of the business, by regulation and law, are pretty much beyond anything else you could imagine," Elward says. "I remember working seven months in a row without a day off, including Sundays."

After an uneventful first year, problems began to develop at Palisades. In January 1973, the plant was forced to shut down for two months after pinhole-size leaks developed in the steam generator tubes, resulting in a small leak of radioactive water. Palisades operated just six months after that problem was corrected before

another leak was found, shutting the plant for more than a year. The plant finally reopened in August 1974, but it only managed to stay operational for three weeks before water leaks in the condenser forced yet another shutdown.

This unpleasant cycle of shutdowns and restarts continued through the 1970s and beyond. Consumers Power settled a safety-regulation fine with the Nuclear Regulatory Commission (NRC), successor to the AEC, in 1974 for $225,000. That same year, the company sued Bechtel, builder of the Palisades plant, and several suppliers of components for $300 million, alleging they used defective equipment.

Palisades Nuclear Plant was projected as an economic windfall for Michigan. But the plant was plagued with problems over the next 30-plus years.

"Our whole mantra had been scraping and saving money, and then we could do anything we wanted after Midland got done."

Consumers Power and Bechtel settled out of court seven years later for $14 million, but the trouble at Palisades was far from over. The plant would be subject to frequent shutdowns and additional NRC fines for the next three decades.

Despite the unsteady start at Palisades, Consumers Power was committed to an even bigger nuclear project: a two-unit, 1,300-megawatt plant near the town of Midland. When plans for the project were first announced in

1967, its estimated total cost was $349 million. The price tag ultimately rose to more than 10 times that amount, nearly doing what two wars and the Great Depression had been unable to do—bankrupt Consumers Power.

A SHAKY FOUNDATION
The concept behind the Midland Nuclear Power Plant was unique: it was to be the world's first cogenerating nuclear plant. Cogeneration is

the simultaneous production of electricity and steam from a single fuel–typically, natural gas, coal, wood or biomass, but nuclear can work, as well. The steam and electricity are used in industrial processes, while excess power is sold to local utility customers. Midland would be designed to produce steam to feed the enormous appetite of a Dow Chemical plant across the Tittawabassee River while generating inexpensive electricity for Consumers Power's other retail and commercial customers.

Dave Joos, former CEO and chairman of the board of Consumers Energy, recalls, "There was a great deal of sophisticated, first-of-its-kind engineering involved in transferring the flow of steam from one unit to another if one shut down–doing that very quickly, and at the same time not disturbing the normal function of the nuclear plant. While the Bechtel design made that happen, the nuclear safety systems were so sensitive that they'd cause the unit to trip every time."

The underlying complexity of the design was only the beginning of the challenges facing the Midland project. The building designed to contain the plant's diesel generator was sinking and cracking because the soil had not been properly compacted.

Consumers Power hired Ralph Brazelton Peck, the country's leading soil engineer, to propose a solution to the unstable soil, but the plan didn't satisfy the NRC. Ultimately, an elaborate and expensive tunneling system was required to shore up the building's foundation.

Meanwhile, the growing anti-nuclear movement, virtually silent during the building of Big Rock Point in the 1960s, had found its voice in the person of Midland resident Mary Sinclair. A former technical writer for the Atomic Energy Commission and Dow Chemical, Sinclair led opposition to the plant, writing letters to the editor of the *Midland Daily News* that questioned the plant's safety and rallied the public behind her cause.

Protesters became a regular presence at the construction site as well as at Consumers Power's public meetings. Sinclair debated the

safety of nuclear power with Consumers Power's Senior Vice President Russell Youngdahl in 1974; the debate was broadcast nationally by PBS, giving opponents of the project great visibility at a time when nuclear power had become a hot-button issue.

THE GROUND REALLY SHIFTS

In the 1980s, Consumers Power had placed all its bets on Midland, and making the investment to complete the plant was the singular focus of Consumers Power leadership. The company had originally informed Dow Chemical, which was to have been the plant's largest customer, that Midland would be operational by 1979 or 1980. The contract obligated Consumers Power to begin supplying Dow with steam by 1982. Slow, costly progress ensued, but time was slipping before the first fuel was supposed to be loaded, and the company's costs had ballooned to more than $1.5 billion.

In a move to accelerate progress, John Selby, who had been president and CEO of Consumers Power for about a year, assigned Tom Elward to be Midland's plant manager in 1978. Elward had held management positions at both Palisades and Big Rock Point, becoming something of a "super problem solver" at both nuclear facilities. Chief among his achievements was getting Big Rock Point restarted after problems with the reactor depressurization system. The plant ended up running continuously for a then-world record 343 days.

Armed with a fax machine, photocopier and a network of activists, former Dow technical researcher Mary Sinclair spearheaded opposition that—along with construction problems and a ballooning price tag—helped sink the Midland Nuclear Plant, shown opposite at about 8o percent complete.

Dave Joos, seen below in the 1980s, worked at the Midland Nuclear Power Plant during construction in the 1970s. Cost overruns at Midland and new federal regulations issued after the accident at Pennsylvania's Three Mile Island nuclear plant threatened to cripple Consumers Power. Joos left the company in 1979 and returned four years later to oversee a review of Midland and help the company decide what to do with the plant. He eventually became president and CEO, streamlining operations and leading a reinvestment in the utility.

At Midland, Elward says, "When I came on board ... the schedule said we were to load fuel in 1981, which meant we had three years to hire a vast array of people to run this complex plant, and put them through the required licensing and certifications." The plant comprised 200 different systems, and each needed its own operating procedures, training programs and licensure requirements before the NRC would approve fuel loading. It was a daunting challenge, but Elward believed it could be done.

Then, just before dawn on March 28, 1979, a pressure valve malfunctioned at the Three Mile Island Nuclear Generating Station near Harrisburg, Pa. A series of failures—technical problems, human error and bad luck—combined to cause the worst nuclear accident in U.S. history. Contaminated water leaked from the nuclear core into an adjoining building and started to release radioactive gases, causing the plant's supervisor to declare the first, and to date only, general emergency at an American nuclear facility.

Metropolitan Edison, the plant's operator, was able to stabilize the system, and no injuries or deaths have been connected to the accident. Nevertheless, some 140,000 people were evacuated, a fearful nation demanded greater oversight of the industry, and the political and regulatory ground for nuclear power had shifted forever.

As news of the accident spread, Dave Joos knew that Midland would be in trouble. Three Mile Island and Midland were sister pressurized water reactors, and Joos had recently returned from Pennsylvania, where he had witnessed Three Mile Island's startup procedure in preparation for Midland's.

Immediately after the accident, the NRC instituted regulatory reforms, including a stricter licensing process for new nuclear plants and upgraded requirements for plant design and for equipment such as piping systems, auxiliary feedwater systems, containment building isolation, reliability of pressure relief valves and electrical circuit breakers. It also demanded automated shutdown capabilities.

Midland was about 83 percent complete, and the cost overruns—Consumers Power had by now sunk nearly $2 billion into the plant—were having serious financial repercussions in Jackson.

Joos recalls, "It was clear to me that retrofitting a plant that was already several years behind schedule could be crippling for a company that was already facing cash flow challenges. Those of us in operations were waiting for a power plant that wasn't going to arrive for a very long time, if at all."

ALL HANDS ON DECK

The risk to the company of further delays at Midland was apparent, and the word from the top, Joos says, was "all hands on deck. Completing Midland is the only thing that matters." Frustrated with his assignment to operation of a plant that was far from completion, Joos left Consumers Power in 1979 to take a job with engineering, consulting and construction company Black and Veatch. As Joos moved on, many areas of Consumers Power were cutting costs to "feed the monster," according to Frank Johnson, then-regional general manager.

"Every so often, Midland would run out of money, and there would be a call to reduce costs and preserve cash," recalls Johnson, who joined the company as a meter reader, worked his way up to the executive suite and retired in 2010 as senior vice president of energy operations.

"Those of us outside of nuclear hated the nuclear plants, especially Midland."

Consumers Power had been in strong financial shape in the 1950s and 1960s, its electric and gas revenues increasing significantly thanks in large part to expansion of the residential and industrial belt around Detroit. There was no question that new generation capacity was needed, but, like Johnson, many employees at Consumers Power's fossil-fuel and other plants felt that placing so much of the company's supply bet on Midland was a mistake.

Johnson, whose territory included the residences of many state legislators and members of the public service commission, knew customers' opinions of a utility's performance are based on the service they get. With Midland dragging the company down, some very important people weren't getting very good service—and Johnson was getting an earful.

Without enough money or time to build new electric substations at a pace that could meet demand, Johnson and his team were forced to find creative solutions. Johnson says, "We'd split a circuit in half and put an automatic flow-over switch in the middle, and feed it from two directions. If there was a problem either way, you wouldn't lose the whole circuit, you'd just lose half of it."

Dave Joos returned to Consumers Power in 1983, and his boss, Tom Elward, promptly sent him to Midland to conduct an independent review of progress toward completing the plant. The findings were discouraging.

"The project was still estimated to be about 83 percent complete, which is exactly what we'd been saying in 1979," Joos recalls. Four years and hundreds of millions of dollars had gotten the project no closer to completion, and the company was still pouring an average of about a million dollars a day into Midland.

CEO John Selby commissioned another team to conduct a higher-level, top-down management review of the plant to understand how its construction was being planned, executed and controlled. Paul Elbert, an industrial and labor relations expert, led Selby's

review team. Elbert had skillfully changed the culture of some Consumers Power's regional offices to improve collaboration and reduce antagonism between labor and management. The team discovered that the project's ambitious schedule, which had called for completion of the plant in 1985–already a major delay from original plans by which it was to have been finished five years earlier–required a prescription for rose-colored glasses.

"It was a presentation of a construction dream rather than a reality," says Elbert, who would later become president and CEO of the company's natural gas business. "Everything was based on the best-case scenario rather than on a reasonable schedule attached to realistic goals and objectives. When you put pressure on employees to meet unreasonable schedules, what do you get? You get errors, and when you have the NRC all over you, it's going to bite you. And it did."

With the NRC issuing a blizzard of stop-work orders on the Midland project, the team presented its grim findings to Selby.

"We were already into this plant to the tune of $4.1 billion, which was an awful lot of money for a company of the size we were in the early 1980s," says Joos. Consumers Power couldn't continue throwing good money after bad. Indeed, good or bad, there was no more money to throw. Consumers Power's credit rating had been downgraded multiple times, capital had dried up, and the state and customers had no appetite for allowing the company to raise its rates. In fact, a coalition of Consumers Power's largest industrial customers called upon the MPSC to reject a plan for a series of rate increases aimed at paying for the plant.

"We couldn't possibly raise what we needed to finish the project," Joos says.

To make matters worse, Detroit Edison—Michigan's second-largest power company, whose rates exceeded those of Consumers Power—was on target to finish its Fermi 2 nuclear plant by 1986. DTE Energy hadn't had the kind of problems with Fermi that Consumers Power had with Midland, and the MPSC decided Michigan didn't need as much power as the two

Construction workers at the Midland Nuclear Plant head home after a day of work in May 1984. Two months later, Midland's 4,000 workers left the nuclear plant site for good after then-Consumers Power Chairman John Selby ordered the project shut down.

nuclear plants would generate. There was little support anywhere for Midland.

Then the ground *really* came out from under the project. On July 15, 1983, Dow Chemical, after years of complaining about the plant's slow progress, terminated its cogeneration contract and sued Consumers Power for negligence, seeking $60 million in damages. Dow claimed that Consumers Power had misled it about the project's timeline for years.

HITTING BOTTOM

Reality finally sank in at the highest levels of the company. On July 16, 1984, Consumers Power's board of directors voted unanimously to pull the plug on Midland. After devouring nearly 20 years and half of the company's assets, Midland was shut down, and its employees were sent home.

Carolyn Bloodworth, now the director of corporate giving and secretary/treasurer of the Consumers Energy Foundation, was fresh out of college then and was one of a small handful of people from the Jackson office temporarily working at Midland to help with construction scheduling.

"On the day they announced the shutdown, I was working in a trailer out on the perimeter

of the property, and I started hearing a thump, thump, thump sound," she recalls. "I went to the window and saw contractors throwing tools over the security fence. That was my first clue that something was wrong."

Bloodworth still had a job, but others weren't as fortunate. "That was a very emotional time," she says. "People had a lot of pride in the work they had been doing for a long time, and they had no idea what they would do now."

The uncertainty spread far beyond the company's Midland employees. Richard Ford, who retired in 2014 as Consumers Energy's vice president of transmission, recalls where he was when he heard the news.

"I was on vacation, and heard it on the radio," he says. "Our whole mantra had been scraping and saving money, and then we could do anything we wanted after Midland got done. When it got shut down, we didn't know if the company itself would be stable much longer. We were all wondering if we should leave, and a lot of people did. They didn't want to hang around and wait for the ax to fall."

Among those who were leaving was John Selby.

The chief of staff of the Michigan Public Service Commission was the first public figure to call for the embattled CEO's resignation. The full commission followed in March 1985 with a statement that it was "imperative that the board replace Mr. Selby with a manager equipped to deal effectively with changed circumstances."

Financially, the company was a mess. Consumers Power had stopped paying dividends to stockholders in the fourth quarter of 1984; it was the first time since 1913 that the company had missed a dividend payment. By January 1985, Consumers Power's share price had dropped to $4.13—down from $20 per share three years earlier. The company was so close to defaulting on its major debt that General Motors agreed to pay its September electric bill early so Consumers Power could make a debt-service payment. With the company's credit at its lowest point and no cash on hand—

all of it had been plowed into the failed Midland venture—Consumers Power desperately needed a rate increase if it had any hope of survival. Without it, "We would have been the first utility to file Chapter 11 bankruptcy since the Great Depression," says Dan Bishop, Consumers Energy's director of media relations.

FIGHTING FOR SURVIVAL

To save itself, the company restructured the nearly $1.2 million in unsecured loans it had accumulated and pledged not to resume construction at Midland. That stemmed the bleeding, but it did nothing to pay down the mountain of debt nor to resolve the looming Dow Chemical lawsuit. A judgment against Consumers Power in the $60 million case could put Consumers Power right back on the edge.

What Consumers Power desperately needed was new leadership—someone who could pull it out of the post-Midland morass and set it on a course back to profitability, reliability and respect. The board of directors found its candidate in William ("Bill") McCormick, a sophisticated and intellectual nuclear engineer educated at the Massachusetts Institute of Technology.

McCormick was a Washington, D.C., man. He'd begun his career at the Institute for Defense Analysis and was eventually appointed by President Gerald Ford to join the White House Energy Policy Office, just as the oil embargo was getting underway. There was no U.S. Department of Energy in those days, so the 27-year-old McCormick was one of a handful of people informally setting United States energy policy. After Ford's defeat in 1976, McCormick moved into energy lobbying, pushing for deregulation of natural gas for the American Gas Association, and then to the Detroit-based natural gas transmission and storage company American Natural Resources (ANR).

While he had little operating experience, McCormick brought a level of political savvy that the company would need if it hoped to repair its reputation.

McCormick was named Consumers Power's chairman and president on Nov. 1, 1985. He

set to work immediately trying to restore the company's tattered business, battered image and demoralized workforce. He brought new policy, industry and technical experts into the company; met with members of Michigan's state legislature and U.S. congressional delegation; commissioned a study to evaluate options for salvaging something from the Midland debacle; and went on a communications blitz to tell a new story of the company's pending renaissance.

In many camps, McCormick's presence was seen as a breath of fresh air, his message as one that made sense. In March 1986, the *Detroit Free Press* wrote, "The leadership of the troubled utility company has been given new life and verve in the person of William T. McCormick, whose preoccupation is not with the disaster of the past but with the future–that of the utility itself and Michigan's energy needs in the last decade and a half of this century."

McCormick promised to restore Consumers Power's credit rating, reverse its declining stock prices, navigate a course out of the legal problems with Dow and bring the company back to life. Those were big promises, to be sure, and for a brief, heady time, McCormick was able to do all that and more.

Consumers Power was in dire shape in 1985 when nuclear engineer Bill McCormick was tapped as its new CEO. With strong political connections and experience in almost every aspect of the energy business— pipelines, distribution, oil and gas, and coal— McCormick seemed prepared to guide the company back to prosperity.

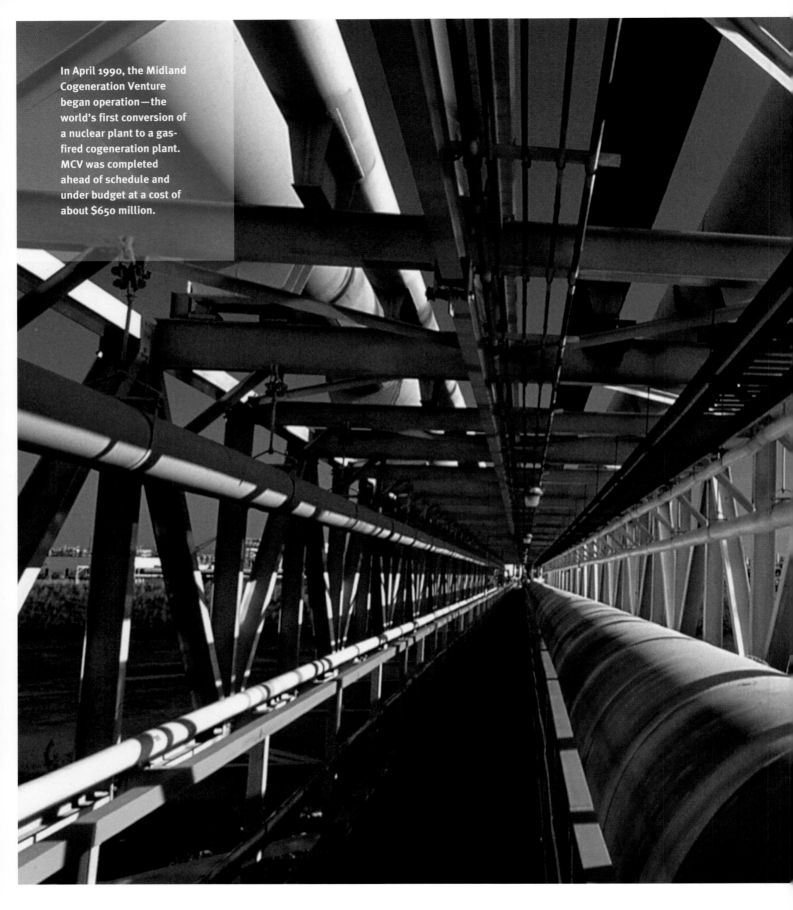

In April 1990, the Midland Cogeneration Venture began operation—the world's first conversion of a nuclear plant to a gas-fired cogeneration plant. MCV was completed ahead of schedule and under budget at a cost of about $650 million.

4: Count on Us

"WANT TO BUY SOME STEAM?"

The handwritten note from Consumers Power Chairman and President Bill McCormick, at the bottom of a letter to a Dow Chemical vice president, was the first visible sign that McCormick had not given up on the failed Midland nuclear plant. Public sentiment was in favor of abandoning the site altogether, but McCormick was determined to try to redeem the $4 billion investment in Midland, which had swallowed some 45 percent of the company's assets.

His motivation was not just that the company had sunk so much of its net worth into a project that had generated nothing in return; Consumers Power desperately needed the power. With electric sales growing, the company was starved for new generating capacity, especially with the 1,300 megawatts Consumers Power had expected from the Midland plant never coming online. Michigan's projected needs put the company in a 1,000-megawatt deficit by 1995.

McCormick formed a team to look into alternatives for Midland. James Cook, who had been vice president of construction for the nuclear plant, led what was called the Midland Options Study, using sophisticated computer models and analytics. The group's work took five months.

Several possibilities were on the table as the team began: scrap the plant altogether, convert it to coal, try yet again to complete it as a nuclear plant—an idea almost certainly destined to fail—or revisit the facility's original cogeneration concept minus the nuclear power source. In the spring of 1986, the study group recommended that Midland be converted into a natural gas, combined-cycle cogeneration plant. Management agreed.

On Monday, April 7, 1986, in back-to-back press conferences in Detroit and Lansing, McCormick stood beside poster-sized photos of the abandoned Midland site and asked, rhetorically, "Given that the company and the state will need more generating capacity; given that the company is financially handicapped because of a large, non-producing asset; and

At full capacity, the Midland cogeneration plant could produce up to 1,500 megawatts of electricity and 1.35 million pounds per hour of industrial steam.

Pete Lehman, vice president and Michigan general manager of Dow Chemical USA, left, and Consumers Power Chairman and President Bill McCormick address reporters in a September 1986 press conference. Their announcement that Dow Chemical and Consumers Power would resume their partnership with Midland as a cogeneration plant ended years of acrimony between the companies over the project.

given that this asset can provide the electricity needed by the company and the state—given all that, doesn't common sense suggest that the Midland asset should be put to work?"

McCormick then described plans for the Midland Cogeneration Venture (MCV), centered around a retrofitted Midland plant. MCV would comprise eight combined-cycle units, each consisting of a gas turbine, an electrical generator and a boiler-like device called a heat recovery steam generator. Air entering each turbine would be pressurized, mixed with natural gas and ignited, producing temperatures in excess of 2,000 degrees Fahrenheit. The energy would turn the turbines, generating electricity. As exhaust left the turbines, it would still be hot enough—about 1,000 degrees—to produce steam by heating water that ran through pipes within the heat recovery steam generators. The steam would drive another turbine and generator, producing more electricity before being condensed to water and recycled.

Midland's skeleton, idle on the bank of the Tittawabassee River, already held one gas turbine and electrical generator, requiring that seven new systems be procured. Other remnants of the plant could be repurposed, as

well: the administration and turbine buildings, two warehouses, the cooling pond, the control room and main plant transformers. Even with all that recycling, the plant was projected to take four years to build and cost about $434 million—money that Consumers Power emphatically did not have.

TOGETHER AGAIN

Of course, in order to work as a cogeneration project, Midland would need a major industrial customer for its output. With few qualified candidates nearby, Consumers Power had but one option: go back to its erstwhile partner, Dow Chemical, with which it had been entangled in a contentious lawsuit over the Midland nuclear failure for three years.

"Dow had a pretty lousy feeling about Consumers Power," says Carl English, a 35-year company veteran who served as executive vice president, president and CEO of Consumers Power's gas unit. But Dow was having problems of its own, and MCV offered a way out of them. As English explains, "Dow had been depending on our steam, and the delays with Midland meant they had to produce their own, using some aged plants on site that weren't ideal."

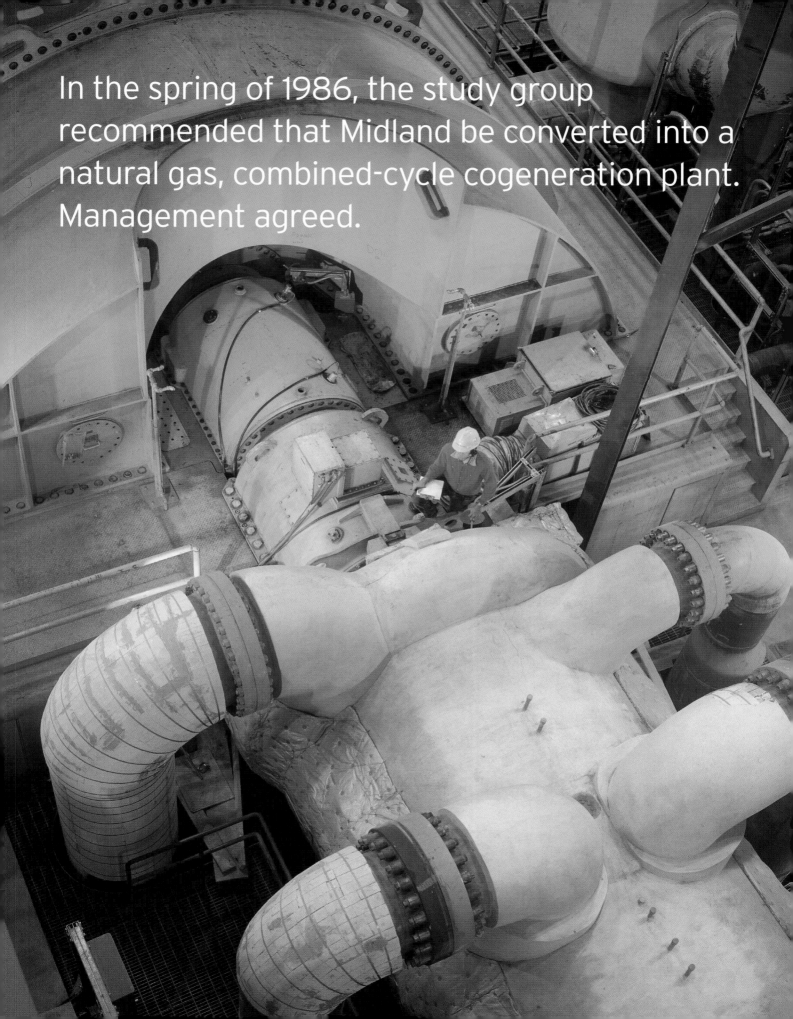

In the spring of 1986, the study group recommended that Midland be converted into a natural gas, combined-cycle cogeneration plant. Management agreed.

In January 1987, executives of Dow Chemical and Consumers Power signed the documents establishing the Midland Cogeneration Venture, below. They later wore baseball caps with MCV logos to greet the press.

The newfound mutual interests brought the estranged partners back together. In September 1986, four months after McCormick had made the plans for MCV public, Dow Chemical and Consumers Power announced an agreement in principle to work together to convert a portion of the idled nuclear plant into a cogeneration facility and to settle their legal differences. Dow would drop its lawsuit, be the plant's primary customer for power and invest in the project as a limited-equity partner.

McCormick and Pete Lehman, vice president and Michigan general manager of Dow Chemical USA, beamed as they told reporters that, when it opened in 1990, MCV would be the first facility of its kind in the nation and the largest in the world. It would generate the same 1,300 megawatts of electricity that the nuclear plant was to have produced, plus 600,000 pounds of steam per hour for Dow's Michigan Division, which develops specialty chemicals for automotive, agricultural, paper, pharmaceutical and bioscience applications. Dow would use about 75 percent of the plant's electricity, while the remainder would be sold to Consumers

Power. McCormick and Lehman said they would jointly ask the Michigan Public Service Commission to remove restrictions placed on Consumers Power's ability to spend money on the abandoned facility.

"It was a real turnaround for the relationship between the two companies when the partnership was announced," says English.

By January 1987, the agreement in principle became an agreement in fact, as Dow and representatives of Consumers Power signed more than two dozen documents finalizing a complex transaction—with equally complicated regulatory implications—creating the Midland Cogeneration Venture Limited Partnership (MCV). Consumers Power and Dow Chemical were the largest investors in MCV. A Dow unit called Rofan Energy Inc. invested $115 million in cash and received a minority interest while Consumers Power, through various subsidiaries, put up $1.5 billion of its Midland assets and received a 49 percent equity stake along with interest-bearing notes totaling $1.27 billion.

Michigan Gov. James Blanchard, U.S. Sen. Carl Levin of Michigan, a great number of

industry analysts and many local and industry media praised the deal. Some 90 positive editorials appeared in newspapers statewide.

"Consumers Power managed to take something that looked like a good idea in principle and deliver on it," declared *Energy Daily*. "TRUCE!" trumpeted the *Detroit News*. Gushed the *Muskegon Chronicle*, "Good news for all of Michigan."

Not everyone was so enthusiastic, however. For one thing, Consumers Power required approval from the Michigan Public Service Commission to recover the cost of purchasing power from MCV in its rates, and the utility wasn't exactly in its good graces. There also was the matter that building a natural gas-fueled power plant at the time was against federal law.

THE PURPOSE OF PURPA
Back in 1978, during the height of the post-OPEC-embargo energy crisis, Congress had passed the Power Plant and Industrial Fuel Use Act. Because of the shortage of fossil fuels, it banned the use of natural gas to power large generating stations.

Consumers Power had a way around that challenge, however—paradoxically, another 1978 energy law designed to spur quick development of alternatives to oil-fired generation, reduce demand for fossil fuels and encourage competition. Known as the Public Utilities Regulatory Policy Act of 1978 (PURPA), the law sought to create a market for nontraditional sources of energy such as renewables. It did that while also breaking open utilities that had essentially been closed markets.

As former Consumers Power lawyer Ted Vogel explains, "We were all vertically integrated, from the power plant to the customer—generation to transmission and distribution. Some utilities even bought coal mines, so they literally had the entire business to themselves, from taking the coal out of the ground to moving it to burning it. Nobody could force a utility to buy electricity from anybody else. PURPA was one of the first cracks in that wall."

Before PURPA, only utilities could own and

operate generating plants and sell electricity to the public. PURPA simultaneously permitted a new class of non-utility power plants and required utilities to buy power from these new independent companies at a price equal to the utilities' "avoided costs"—that is, the amount a utility would have had to spend to generate the power itself or buy it from another source. Under PURPA, two kinds of generating facilities were singled out for special rate and regulatory treatment: plants fueled by renewable sources and cogeneration. These were called Qualifying Facilities, or QFs.

"The law was really intended to promote smaller plants burning unique fuels, like waste woods, and give them competitive rates for their power," Vogel says. Although many believed the law hadn't been intended to encourage the development of behemoths like a 1,300-megawatt plant burning natural gas, the proposed MCV did meet PURPA's requirements for a QF.

Consumers Power didn't have enough cash on hand to buy a $400-million-plus steam plant, and Dow Chemical wasn't inclined to pay the full cost. For those reasons, and to enable the plant to qualify under PURPA rules, the companies established MCV as an independent, privately owned facility, with Consumers Power and Dow retaining large equity positions (the law did

Consumers Power employees had reason to celebrate at this centennial picnic in Jackson in July 1986: after several tough years, the company appeared headed in the right direction.

Keeping the Power On

An employee helps restore power in Kalamazoo after an ice storm, opposite, in 2011. Below, in 2012, the company launched its Enhanced Infrastructure Replacement Project (EIRP), a major initiative to accelerate replacement of natural gas pipeline throughout its service territory. The program involves replacing about 3,200 miles of pipeline over 25 years—work that otherwise would have taken 75 years.

Beginning on December 21, 2013, households all across Michigan were battered by a crippling swath of ice, snow and freezing rain that swept across the state. Ice storms during the early part of the week were followed by several inches of blowing snow on Christmas Eve. More than 10,600 wires toppled, and 400,000 people—nearly 23 percent of Consumers Energy's customers—were left without power, some literally just as they were about to put their holiday dinners in the oven. It was the largest Christmas week storm in the company's history and the largest storm it had faced in a decade.

Consumers Energy was ready to respond. Between 2009 and 2014, the company invested nearly $400 million to upgrade and modernize its electric distribution system. The work included inspecting and replacing poles and cross-arms, clearing lines, and replacing transformers and wires. Without the upgrades, many more customers would almost certainly have been without power.

By Christmas morning, power outages had been cut to just over 100,000. Three days later, only 18,000 households remained without power, thanks to extensive preparation, round-the-clock work, and aid from mutual assistance crews from 13 states and Washington, D.C.

In the aftermath of the storm, Consumers Energy's customer satisfaction rates increased.

"It was the biggest storm many of us had seen in our professional careers, and our response and our communication were so good that customer satisfaction actually improved," says President and CEO Patti Poppe.

By 2014, even with severe storms punctuating the region's summer and winter weather, almost 98 percent of customers saw their power restored in 36 hours or less, no matter how extreme the conditions.

The company continues to invest about $150 million per year to upgrade and modernize its electric distribution system—in addition to the $45 million it spends annually on line-clearing work to enhance reliability and reduce tree and vegetation contact with electric lines.

Investing in reliability is essential to the natural gas system, too. Between 2014 and 2016, Consumers Energy spent more than $500 million on improvements throughout Lower Michigan, replacing infrastructure, upgrading compressor and pressure regulation facilities, and accommodating new business and residential customer growth. Miles of pipeline were replaced with plastic and steel to improve gas deliverability and reliability, and pipeline systems were augmented with new natural gas compressor and regulation facilities.

Consumers Power's Women's Advisory Panel, in a 1987 meeting, right, was one of the first of a series of Employee Resource Groups designed to foster an inclusive workplace. Other groups include the Women's Engineering Network, the Minority Advisory Panel, the Hispanic Outreach Team and the Veterans Advisory Panel.

not allow either company to have a controlling interest) and outside investors pitching in.

John Clark, a former colleague of Bill McCormick from the U.S. Department of Energy who was the first person the CEO hired when he joined Consumers Power, recalls that "getting approval for MCV under PURPA was a ferociously political process.

"Many people wanted us to bury Midland and start elsewhere," says Clark, former senior vice president for communications. "They were so tired of the controversy, and it had so poisoned our relationships with the state. They wanted us to just let this thing lie and not resurrect it."

The Michigan Public Service Commission was hearing from industrial customers and consumer advocates deeply opposed to Consumers Power's request to recover the costs of the power purchased from the cogeneration facility in its rates. That would raise average rates about 15 percent.

Overcoming that obstacle took almost two years, according to Mike Morris, another early McCormick recruit—they'd worked together at American Natural Resources. Morris was hired as senior vice president of natural gas, but McCormick realized that Morris' longstanding positive relationship with the MPSC could help move Midland forward. McCormick put Morris in charge of shepherding MCV's power cost

recovery through the regulatory process.

Even with Morris' connections and good reputation, that wasn't easy.

"At one point, we had been reporting to the board for months on end that we would get this deal done," Morris says. "All parties involved had agreed to the settlement. We finally made the filing, and the MPSC agreed to hear the case directly—normally, there would be a hearing examiner or judge to hear the case. After all the testimony, the chair of the commission said that parts of the settlement were completely unacceptable, and they rejected it out of hand."

Stunned, Morris walked out of the hearing. He sat in the hallway for a few minutes, collecting himself, before the MPSC's chief of staff walked up to him and noted how disappointed he must be.

"Shocked would be more accurate," Morris retorted. "We were in dialogue for weeks, and we thought you were in agreement with the outline we had."

The chief of staff said the settlement hadn't been rejected forever and that Morris should expect to get a call in a few days.

Sure enough, within a week, Morris was called to come back to the commission to start the process again. This time, Consumers Power proposed restructuring the deal so that it yielded about $100 million less for shareholders, putting that money back in the pockets of customers in the form of lower rates.

MCV began commercial operation in 1990 and ultimately proved capable of generating up to 1,500 megawatts of electricity and up to 1.35 million pounds per hour of industrial steam. The plant operated under shared company ownership until 2006, when in an environment of sustained high natural gas prices, Consumers Energy sold its 49 percent stake in the venture to GSO Capital Partners LP and Rockland Capital Energy Investments for $60.5 million. The company, which used the proceeds to pay down debt, continued to purchase electricity from the plant and was still doing so in 2016.

CASHING IN BILLY BUCKS

Fortunately for Consumers Power, even as the regulatory process for Midland dragged on, market conditions had improved to such a degree that the utility was already turning a financial corner. The recession that hit Michigan so hard in the early 1980s eased, unemployment rates were down, consumer spending was on the rise, automakers were profitable again and demand for power was strong.

New service requests for the first six months of 1986 shot up 31 percent for natural gas and 30 percent for electricity, with total electricity sales up 1.7 percent. By July, Consumers Power reported a significant improvement in second-quarter earnings over the previous year. Though profitability was still a distant dream, net losses were down to $6 million from $22.5 million in the second quarter the year before.

Trying to keep costs low without completely demoralizing an already beleaguered workforce, the company instituted a novel salary reduction program that reduced operating expenses while ultimately benefiting employees handsomely. Salaries were cut across the board, but Consumers Power put "shares of stock" equal in value to the difference between each employee's previous compensation and their new, lower pay into a dedicated fund. The shares were indexed to the depressed value of Consumers Power's stock at the time the program began. Pay increases were awarded but not actually paid

out; that money, too, went into the fund in the form of stock. Eventually, employees called the money set aside "Billy Bucks," in a reference to McCormick.

"It was like forced savings, but it also gave us an incentive to help the company get back on its feet," says Fern Griesbach, who retired in 2016 as Consumers Energy's executive director of human resources. "I had only been with the company for three years, but I still had the sense that I was part of the solution."

The sacrifice by employees strengthened the company's cash position and enabled Consumers Power to eke ever closer to profitability, and by January 1988, the Billy Bucks had paid off for employees: they received all of their back pay, with healthy bonuses on top driven by a six-fold increase in Consumers Power's stock price.

"The stock went from $3 to $18 a share when it paid out," Griesbach says. "People did really well. I heard stories of many employees paying their kids' college tuition with the appreciation of the stock during those years."

THE NIGHT STALKER

If Consumers Power were to truly restore morale, it would take more than money. After all, for many utility employees, their work is more than a job; it's a way of life. It's about being part of a tight-knit team on a mission to get the lights on and to safely and reliably keep them on—and on those counts, the company had faltered.

As efforts to keep Midland a going concern became management's key focus, bedrock priorities such as workplace safety, customer service and management-labor cooperation had taken a back seat. That was painfully obvious to Paul Elbert, the former Midland review team leader, in 1986 when he was assigned to become general manager of the Karn-Weadock fossil-fuel complex in Bay City. He witnessed testy exchanges between managers and union members, and on several occasions, acts of work disruption and vandalism clearly aimed at showing those at the top how little employees felt heard.

Elbert decided it was time to change things.

Environmental Stewardship

Only a small portion of the land that the Karn-Weadock fossil-fuel plant occupied near Bay City was needed for generating electricity in the mid-1980s, the rest being a buffer between the plant and the community. Recognizing that hundreds of acres of mostly waterfront property on Saginaw Bay held significant environmental potential, Consumers Power asked the Michigan Audubon Society to lead an effort to transform 900 acres of plant property to be more environmentally friendly.

Waterfront development planned for downtown Bay City was going to disturb a nesting site of the common tern, and it was a priority for the society to provide the birds with new habitat to compensate for the loss. In spite of their name, common terns are all but common in Michigan. Once numbering more than 6,000 breeding pairs, the birds

were down to only 2,000 pairs—the effect of contaminants, loss of habitat and predators. Michigan listed the birds as a threatened species.

Consumers Power and the Audubon Society established the tern nesting site on two acres of remote property, protected from disturbance, in 1988. Elbert challenged his superintendents to come up with more environmental-improvement projects they could take on with the Audubon Society. Union employees and managers responded by generating dozens of ideas and donating untold hours of their time, and Karn-Weadock now has bluebird houses, osprey nests, a raptor rehabilitation center, a butterfly garden and a nature trail. About 140 bird species and innumerable woodland and wetland mammals live on or visit the site.

Karn-Weadock is one of many

For more than 20 years, employees at the Karn-Weadock generating complex have teamed with a local wildlife rehabilitation specialist to nurse hundreds of raptors such as bald eagles back to health in a specially constructed raptor pen. The pen provides room for large birds to fly and rebuild their strength while protected from predators before returning to nature.

environmental success stories at the company, which has earned a reputation as a good environmental steward in its 130 years of serving Michigan. The lands surrounding Consumers Energy's fossil-fuel, hydroelectric and renewable energy operations are home to many plant wildlife habitat protection projects.

Employees at the Whiting coal-fired plant on the Lake Erie shore created a wildflower meadow and a pond filled with the American lotus, Michigan's official symbol of clean water. An Eagle Scout named Matthew Netherland built 22 bat boxes out of scrap Chevrolet Volt battery covers donated by General Motors, and Consumers Energy installed them near its hydroelectric dams, providing homes for more than 100 bats per box.

Protected nesting areas for bald eagles established on company property along rivers in the Lower Peninsula have helped bring the number of nesting pairs back from just six in the late 1970s to a record 750 in 2015. Consumers Energy established safe zones around every nest, protected the birds' food supply and added new breeding grounds near many of its historic hydroelectric dams.

"Many of the eagles soaring over Michigan today trace their roots to eagles that nested near Tippy Dam and other hydro facilities Consumers Energy operates along the Manistee, Au Sable and Muskegon rivers," says

Gary Dawson, the company's director of land and water policy.

Before building Lake Winds Energy Park in Mason County, Consumers Energy spent two years studying the potential impact of the wind farm on resident short ear owls, bald eagles and Indiana bats, as well as on songbird breeding and the migration patterns of large birds. Construction began only after the studies provided sufficient evidence that construction and operation of Lake Winds would not negatively affect federally endangered or threatened birds or bat species such as the eastern pipistrelle, and that the 56 wind turbines would have no impact on rare and unique natural features. Lake Winds opened in 2012.

Consumers Energy contributes hundreds of thousands of dollars annually to environmental stewardship efforts and to organizations such as the Detroit River International Wildlife Refuge, the Michigan Department of Natural Resources Wetland Wonders Challenge and the Rouge Education Project, which encourages elementary and high school students to help restore and protect Detroit's Rouge River, one of the most polluted in the nation.

"Our commitment in everything we do is to leave Michigan better than we found it," says John Russell, chairman of the CMS Energy and Consumers Energy boards of directors.

The J.R. Whiting plant, located on an 875-acre site along the Lake Erie shoreline, was certified by the Wildlife Habitat Council every year from 1991 to 2014 for its natural resources stewardship. It held a wildflower meadow and lotus pond, and employees and their families kept the beach clean.

He started coming into the plant at all times of day and night—often during third shift, in the wee hours of the morning. He'd just walk around, talk to employees and watch what was happening. Front-line workers called him the "night stalker." Elbert was earning their respect, and he knew that was a term of affection.

"People liked that I would come in at 2 a.m., a time when they never, ever saw the plant manager, and sit and talk with them," Elbert says.

Elbert did more than make his presence known and give an ear to employees' concerns. He began improving conditions at the plant, gave people power to control their environment and offered them the responsibility to identify and solve problems on their own.

For example, Elbert had been at the plant about two weeks when it dawned on him how dim the lighting was. A remarkable number of fluorescent bulbs were out and hadn't been replaced, and flashlights had become standard issue for maintenance workers. Elbert ordered the superintendents to replace every light bulb within a week.

"I was told they purchased every fluorescent light bulb in Bay County to do that," Elbert says. "Suddenly, you'd walk in and things were bright. You could see."

Employees called many problems to Elbert's attention, among them that the procedure manuals that plant operators and maintenance people relied on had been written by and for engineers. They were full of technical jargon and detail that was irrelevant, incomprehensible and potentially dangerous in the hands of an operator, so they were often ignored.

"We didn't have engineers running the plants. We had operators," Elbert says. "They had tons of experience and knowledge, but it had been gained in highly specific training classes reinforced by learning on the job. We undertook a massive effort to rewrite their operating manuals in the lingo and understanding of the people who actually had to do the job. The result: when you took a procedural guide out, you could follow it without a master's degree in mechanical engineering."

Management supervision at Karn-Weadock

was reduced, and lead union employees were given responsibility for the operation of their areas and the performance they achieved. As Elbert says, "If one of your jobs was to make sure the boiler feed pumps worked and had a low failure rate, it was up to you to understand how to maintain the pumps and to make sure the maintenance was performed. I gave our lead union maintenance employee total responsibility for the performance of the boiler feed pump."

One employee asked Elbert a question that to an outsider might have sounded odd but that made perfect sense to anyone who has ever spent more than a few minutes on a factory or power plant floor—especially one that dates from the 1950s: "Everything in the plant is always painted battleship gray and vomit green," the employee observed. "Can I paint the pump any color I want?"

Sure, Elbert told him, it's yours. The next day, the pump was gleaming gold, with a black dollar sign on it.

"The employee told us that without that boiler feed pump, the power plant doesn't work and the company doesn't make any money," Elbert says. "That's a union employee talking!"

The story of culture change at Karn-Weadock spread quickly throughout Consumers Power, and practices such as those Elbert had pioneered took root in other operations, with similar results.

At the Campbell 3 plant in West Olive, where Steve Van Slooten had started his company career as an unskilled worker in 1981, he and his co-workers welcomed the growing empowerment.

"In the late 1980s, we formed a joint committee to develop a certification program for the unions," says Van Slooten, who by then had become vice president of the local utility workers' union and is now the national vice president of the Utility Workers' Union of America, AFL-CIO. "Operator certification gave our people a lot more training and responsibility. They were able to take more responsibility for their jobs, and the importance of what our people did and how it affected overall generation finally became truly recognized.

Soon, Consumers Power had found a way to drive the gains straight to the bottom line.

Because it was important that the company show customers, shareholders, regulators and others it was serious about improving operating performance and financial returns—and that it was willing to hold managers accountable—Consumers Power created a set of metrics for performance in such areas as safety and reliability. It then tied budget allocations to the results—the better a department's performance, the more money it got when the next budget cycle came around.

Executives and rank-and-file employees alike responded so well to the incentives that companywide improvement came quickly, as did recognition from the industry. In November 1987, *Electric Light and Power* magazine named Consumers Power its Electric Utility of the Year, with the triumphant headline, "A Winner Bounces Back."

At the time Elbert assumed management of Karn-Weadock in 1986, the plant was logging hundreds of employee grievances every year.

Three years later, when he was promoted to vice president of fossil and hydroelectric operations, that number had plummeted to five—and Elbert's solutions-oriented, employee-empowerment approach had woven its way into the company's fabric.

"Within a few years, there was an absolute turnaround," Elbert said. "We were superlative and recognized for it. Year after year, we were among the top three most reliable utilities in the nation, and we won the National Safety Council's top award as the safest major gas and electric utility for 10 years in a row."

By the beginning of the 1990s, Consumers Power had become the leanest major utility in the United States, with an average of 283 customers served per employee, and the efficiency of its fossil-fuel plants was among the highest in the nation. Meanwhile, revenues in 1989 were $2.9 billion, a tick above 1988. The company reinstated its dividend that year, and the stock price rebounded to $40 per share.

Consumers Power had pulled off a classic turnaround. From the back of the pack, it was now at the head of the class.

The dedication of the completed Midland Cogeneration Venture, energized by a fife and drum corps in 1990, heralded a new and prosperous chapter in the nearly century-long life of Consumers Power.

In September 1997, CMS Energy completed a deal for the acquisition and expansion of the Jorf Lasfar coal-fired power plant in Morocco. The plant symbolized the company's global aspirations in the go-go 1990s: at that point, CMS Energy also had operations in Argentina, Australia, Chile, India, Jamaica and the Philippines.

5:

Promise and Peril

Frank Johnson helped launch Consumers Power's South American business in 1996. Among the company's holdings was a 12.7 percent interest in Argentina's Hidroelectrica El Chocon, opposite, a 1,320-megawatt hydroelectric plant.

F

rank Johnson's wife knew he had something up his sleeve when, one day in 1996, he called her at work and offered to take her out to lunch.

"You never take me to lunch," she noted with suspicion. "Either you got fired, or we're moving. Which is it?"

After more than 25 years at Consumers Power—he'd started out as a meter reader in 1970—Johnson had been offered a position as head of the company's nascent South American business in Argentina.

"Where will we be living?" his startled wife asked when they got to lunch. Johnson took out the map to show her, only to realize he'd forgotten the exact location of their new home.

"It's in the north somewhere," he told her. Ten days later, they were on a plane bound for Buenos Aires, where an affiliate of CMS Energy had just acquired a majority stake in Empresa Distribuidora de Electricidad de Entre Rios (EDEERSA), an electric utility serving central Argentina.

What was a company that had spent essentially all of its history providing electricity inside the borders of Michigan doing in South America? The answer lies in Consumers Power's turnaround of the late 1980s and structural changes that were upending U.S. and global energy markets at about the same time.

CHANGES IN THE MARKET

Consumers Power had attracted considerable attention in the late 1980s by way of Bill McCormick's forward-looking management and his none-too-shy approach to public relations. Customers, regulators, industry insiders and shareholders were all watching closely.

As John Clark, the company's then-senior vice president of communications, says, "Our nontraditional approach to traditional utility business problems was praised as the wave of the future. There was a clear contrast between what the company was doing and what, for

example, Detroit Edison was doing. A lot of utilities thought a good media strategy was never showing up in the media. We sought a more visible public profile."

With demand for electricity growing at a rate slightly above the national average, the newly solid Consumers Power could look forward to years of steady growth. But McCormick and others in management felt that would be selling the company short—especially given what was happening in the energy market and how utilities elsewhere were responding.

Beginning in the later years of the Gerald Ford administration and sweeping through the presidencies of Jimmy Carter and Ronald Reagan, an urge took root to deregulate industries that provided the backbone of America's infrastructure. The first major U.S. industry to be at least partly deregulated in this era was freight rail, in 1980, and that was followed by trucking, interstate bus transportation, airlines, natural gas and others. Parallel free-market movements gathered steam in other countries such that by the early 1990s, nations throughout Europe, the Middle East and Far East had privatized their once government-owned utilities.

For many American companies, the appeal of pairing a slow-growth, regulated regional utility with a dynamic, faster-growing international business that was unregulated and had a potentially greater upside was irresistible. Formerly staid utilities—Duke Energy, Entergy and American Electric Power among them—took note of the predicted escalating demand for electricity in developing countries, and they diversified their businesses by acquiring power plants and utility companies overseas.

In the meantime, a change in the makeup of utilities' stock ownership further upset fundamentals in the industry. No longer were utility shareowners primarily individual investors who sought safe dividends and slow, certain appreciation of their holdings. Shares were increasingly held by institutions looking for returns competitive with those of other industries.

"The traditional utility was a heavily regulated paradigm," Clark says. "We did well financially early on in McCormick's tenure for being creative with the Midland Cogeneration Venture and not thinking like classic utility guys. That had brought in a lot of institutional investors who wanted hotter, quicker returns—not just the stable stock price and nice dividend that utilities traditionally delivered."

In 1985, only about 18 percent of Consumers Power's common stock was owned by large institutional investors. Just a year later, that figure had more than doubled, to 42 percent. As Vic Fryling, then Consumers Power's vice president for corporate planning and investor relations, told the company's *Progress* magazine in April 1987, "We're not trading as a utility stock. We're trading as a special situation stock, or what some analysts call a special event stock. We were the 17th best performer on the New York Stock Exchange last year."

For many American companies, the appeal of pairing a slow-growth, regulated regional utility with a dynamic, faster-growing international business that was unregulated and had a potentially greater upside was irresistible.

CREATING A HOLDING COMPANY

McCormick wanted to maintain that kind of performance, and he knew shareholders would demand it. So he set his sights far beyond the borders of Michigan.

"Bill thought we should take our expertise in power and technology and bring it to new markets overseas, as well as buy independent power plants in the U.S.," says Dave Joos. "We had a big transferrable skill set, and we could operate utility-like assets all over the world, add value and make money. There was big competition to do this among lots of utilities."

As a regulated utility, Consumers Power wasn't allowed to own foreign assets, so in 1987 it formed a holding company named CMS Energy Corporation, with subsidiaries in utility and non-utility businesses. CMS Energy established its headquarters in Dearborn, Mich.

The utility side—called Consumers Power—generated, distributed and sold retail electricity to residential, commercial and industrial customers. The utility continued to be regulated by the Michigan Public Service Commission and, in some areas of its business, the Federal Energy Regulatory Commission (FERC). All of Consumers Power's power plants except the Midland Cogeneration Venture, and all of the company's transmission infrastructure stayed in the utility.

All non-utility holdings were rolled into an unregulated CMS Energy subsidiary called CMS Enterprises Company, which was intended to give the company a promising new stream of revenue and profits without putting utility customers' rates at risk. In addition to moving existing businesses such as the oil and gas exploration and production company NOMECO and Consumer Power's share in MCV (which would sell electricity to Consumers Power), CMS Energy created several new units to put the company in new businesses. Among them were CMS Generation Co., through which the company would assemble a portfolio of generating plants and become an independent power producer (IPP) in the United States and around the world, and CMS Marketing, Services and Trading Company, a marketing arm that

bought and sold natural gas, electricity, crude oil and liquefied natural gas, and traded energy futures.

In 1987, McCormick and other utility executives with similar aspirations formed the Utility Working Group to lobby for changes in the Public Utility Holding Company Act (PUHCA), which since 1935 had kept utilities from investing in energy-related businesses and projects outside their geographic service territories and internationally, except qualified generation facilities allowed under the 1978 PURPA law. By 1992, there were some 3,000 IPPs in operation in the United States, generating about 6 percent of the country's power. More important, independently produced power accounted for 39 percent of the new capacity that had come online since 1985, and that helped turn the energy shortage of the 1970s and early 1980s into a temporary glut.

Many utilities, which had signed high-priced, federally mandated contracts to buy power from qualifying facilities at a time when they could charge customers comparably high rates, got caught in a money-losing spiral when the energy surplus sent retail prices plummeting. Lobbying in unison through the Utility Working Group, CMS Energy and other pro-expansion utilities sought greater competition and more natural market forces in wholesale power—and in the

In the mid-1990s, the newly issued common stock in CMS Energy appeared to be a secure and high-return investment.

The Atacama Pipeline in Argentina transported gas from northern Argentina's production fields 585 miles across the Andes Mountains to the Pacific coast of northern Chile, to fuel a CMS Energy power plant. CMS Oil and Gas held major interests in several oil fields in eastern Ecuador's Oriente region, opposite.

Energy Policy Act of 1992, they got many of the changes they wanted.

The law opened wide the competitive door by creating a new class of independent power producers called exempt wholesale generators (EWGs), and it enabled all exempt IPPs to charge market prices instead of "just and reasonable" rates that had been set after exhaustive reviews by state public utility commissioners and the Federal Energy Regulatory Commission. The effect of this was to bring wholesale and retail electricity prices more in line with one another.

The Energy Policy Act also opened up the U.S. transmission system to access by IPPs and allowed holding companies to purchase interests in foreign utility companies and power plants. By the end of 1994, electricity holding companies such as CMS Energy had invested more than $5 billion in foreign utilities and EWGs. Few of them truly understood the markets they were entering or what it took to run a formerly government-owned utility in a foreign country.

BIG BAG OF MONEY

At first, CMS Energy lacked the capital to make significant overseas investments, but in 1993, the MPSC finally signed off on the long-awaited Midland Cogeneration agreement. That allowed Consumers Power to recover from ratepayers and partners the cost of 915 of the 1,240 megawatts of energy it had agreed to buy from MCV—generating a substantial amount of cash that many believed belonged to the utility side of the business.

In May 1993, CMS Energy and a group of independent power producers from the United States and Argentina bid on Centrales Termicas San Nicolas, S.A., a 650-megawatt fossil-fuel plant about 60 miles north of Buenos Aires. Although the bid was successful, the partnership didn't last. CMS Energy later sold its interest in San Nicolas, but it had gained the experience it needed and was on its way to building an enormous international portfolio.

Argentina was the first beachhead. CMS Energy quickly established a substantial foothold there, with ownership interests in

an oil- and natural-gas-fueled plant in the wine-producing Mendoza province and two hydroelectric plants in the Neuquen province further south. The company was also a partner in developing the Atacama Pipeline, a $400 million project to transport Argentine natural gas to northern Chile, and it owned shares in Argentina's Transportadora de Gas del Norte pipeline and in Transportadora de Gas del Mercosur, the Argentine section of a pipeline supplying natural gas to a power plant in southwestern Brazil. The Entre Rios acquisition was one of two transactions CMS Energy completed in Argentina just before Frank Johnson left for Buenos Aires, the other involving a cogeneration project in Ensenada.

Prior to working in South America, Johnson had been lead negotiator in one of Consumers Power's toughest labor negotiations ever. He found that even the drama of a local union president staging a news conference to burn pages of a tentative management-labor agreement paled against the way business was done in Entre Rios.

"The agreement was that we would fix up the utility, the government would have a privatized utility, the service would be reliable and everyone would pay," Johnson says. "But there was a lot of theft. Since it had been government-run, people felt it was okay to steal from the utility because the government was so corrupt."

CMS Energy expected to operate Entre Rios just as it did its U.S. business: if a customer didn't pay his or her bill, the service would be discontinued. That was hardly the way things were done in Argentina, and that was especially problematic for CMS Energy because its largest customer—the government—wasn't paying its bill. It hadn't paid for power when the government owned the utility, and it wasn't about to start with the utility in private hands. Officials figured they had CMS Energy over a barrel: it wouldn't dare shut off services to government buildings such as police, schools, hospitals and the fire department.

"I was meeting two or three times a month with the provincial governor and his cabinet, telling them they had to start paying for their

By the end of 1998, CMS Energy had interests in two plants in India: the GVK Industries gas-fired plant, India's first internationally owned and operated power plant, and GMR Vasavi, above, a diesel-fired 200-megawatt baseload plant in which CMS acquired a 49 percent interest in 1997. Together, those plants totaled 435 megawatts of generating capacity.

electricity. They'd say 'sure, sure'—whatever they had to say to get me out the door," Johnson says. Johnson was prepared to play hardball, however, and he reminded officials that "the governor's mansion, the economy minister's house, the police garage, those are also government buildings. We're going to shut those off, and I suspect your wives will not be very happy."

The governor thought Johnson was bluffing. He was not, and the government buildings went dark as promised.

"It scared people back in Michigan because they were figuring they'd have to get me out of prison," Johnson says. "But within 24 hours, this big bag of money shows up, and we put meters on all their buildings."

ENLISTING THE LOCAL PRIEST

In poorer districts, Johnson and his team took a different approach. There, the thieves weren't well-off government officials callously refusing to pay for their electricity. They were people living in grinding poverty in small communities, literally risking their lives to cadge power for their shacks. Using a dangerous technique that sometimes led to electrocution, people would take a cable attached to a small grappling hook called a cat, throw it over a power line and pull it tight. The cable would pull direct current from the line and could be used to power a stove or lamp.

"We had to figure out a solution so that these people wouldn't have to steal and put their lives at risk," Johnson says. His team calculated the power loads needed by these little communities, and the company ran enough service to power the lamps and cooking stoves they used. "If anyone used more than that, there was a throwover switch that would open outside the community, and the whole community would go dark for the rest of the night."

Johnson's team determined how much each person in the community would have to pay for his or her share of the power—but who would collect the money? Community bosses were too corrupt. The local police were worse. Johnson's brainstorm: the revered local priest.

"Energy losses and theft went from 30 percent to 12 percent, and I was a hero with the priest and the Catholic Church," laughs Johnson, who was named entrepreneur of the year by a local magazine before leaving Entre Rios.

"FROM THE WELLHEAD TO THE BURNER TIP"

International employees such as Johnson had to learn the cultures, rules and regulations—not to mention quirks and caprices—of the power business in many different countries. But they did so, and initially with great financial success.

By 1997, CMS Energy owned $10 billion worth of energy assets in 17 countries on five continents and was developing projects in another seven or eight, and its international investments totaled about $3.5 billion. In the five years between 1993 and 1998, the company's global business grew by a compound annual rate of more than 40 percent, according to McCormick.

During that time, CMS Energy also took its NOMECO subsidiary global and began selling oil and gas on open markets; no longer did it explore and produce only domestically and only for Consumers Power's use. By the mid-1990s, NOMECO had producing wells in the United States, Australia, Colombia, Ecuador, Equatorial Guinea, Congo, Tunisia and New Zealand, and it was generating annual revenue of more than $125 million.

In the meantime, the company had interests in 34 operating plants totaling 7,400 gross megawatts and was the fourth-largest U.S.

developer and operator of independent power projects in the world. In a single decade, CMS Energy had become a major player in national and international energy markets.

In a 1998 interview for the Smithsonian Institution's *Powering a Generation of Change*, a project documenting the history of electrical power restructuring in North America, Bill McCormick showed tremendous pride in what the company had achieved and great confidence in even higher ambitions.

"Our strategy is to be an energy infrastructure company that can build, own and operate energy facilities, and provide energy services in all major growth markets," McCormick said. "That sounds like a big statement, and it is. [W]e're certainly one of the most important energy companies in Latin America right now. We are the largest single investor in Argentina of any kind of U.S. company. We have in operation the first independent power plant in India. We're in the Philippines, Thailand and Indonesia. And we're looking at a number of other countries in south and Southeast Asia. We also have the largest

In 1995, CMS Energy acquired Terra Energy, Ltd., below, a major producer and operator of Antrim natural gas wells in northern Michigan.

independent power plants on three continents: North America, Africa (in Morocco) and in Australia (a 2,000-megawatt plant). We also have gas pipelines on three continents, and storage and processing facilities, and oil and gas exploration all over the world.

"Our plan is really to provide energy capability all the way from the wellhead to the burner tip, because we're in all stages of the energy business," he said. "We're in the production of oil and gas, we're in the pipeline business, we're in the processing business, we're in the power generation business, and we're in the transmission and distribution business."

Wall Street validated this vision, pushing the company's common stock to highs of more than $50 per share in midday trading on three days in November and December 1998.

MEANWHILE, IN MICHIGAN …

Back home, the company continued to face challenges, but the picture was mostly bright. The decade had begun with a rapid run-up in fuel prices as a result of the first Gulf War, but U.S. energy consumption grew steadily, increasing by about 17 percent between 1990 and 2000. Supply was abundant, and most of the nation's gas and electric power infrastructure held excess capacity.

With the unregulated side of CMS Energy's business booming in the new era, the local utility business was undergoing its own structural change. Once-closed territories were opening to competition, utilities had greater choice in suppliers, and customers sought a greater menu of products and services and improved reliability. In recognition of these realities, in 1997 Consumers Power changed its name to Consumers Energy Company, adopted the tagline "Count on Us" and began using a logo that featured a bold green "energy shield."

Mike Morris, then Consumers Energy's president and CEO, explained the change in a corporate newsletter, *Weekly Plus*: "The new identity preserves the widely recognized 'Consumers' name while giving our customers a clearer, more consistent impression of the value-added services we provide—of the innovative

energy solutions we can bring to their homes and businesses. Today, and increasingly in the future, our customers are looking for more holistic solutions to their energy needs, regardless of whether the ultimate solution utilizes gas, electricity or a mixture of both."

Environmental improvements were among Consumers Energy's highest priorities of the decade, as new emissions requirements were imposed on fossil-fuel generating plants in amendments made to the federal Clean Air Act in 1990. The amendments required many utilities to upgrade or retrofit their plants to meet stricter guidelines related to acid rain, urban air pollution and toxic emissions. Consumers Energy spent more than $700 million on emissions-reducing technology over 10 years.

In 1998, the J.R. Whiting plant on the shore of Lake Erie became the first power plant in the state to win the Clean Corporate Citizen designation from the Michigan Department of Environmental Quality. It would continue to earn that award for 11 consecutive years.

CMS Enterprises' portfolio includes the Kalamazoo River Generating Station, opposite, a simple-cycle, natural gas-fired peaking plant capable of generating up to 68 megawatts of electricity. Above, an employee works at CMS Enterprises' Dearborn Industrial Generation (DIG) facility. DIG, which is capable of generating up to 710 megawatts of electricity and more than 1 million pounds per hour of steam, earned the state's Clean Corporate Citizen status in 2010.

Support for Farming Communities

Before there was electricity in rural Michigan, farm families in towns like Frankfort, Brethren and Owendale did all their labor by hand or with horses. Washing clothes usually required a windy day, so the windmill could pump water to be heated on the wood stove in a big copper boiler. When there was no wind, there was no water unless someone pumped it by hand— backbreaking work, especially to draw enough water for both the family and the livestock. Parents read and children did their schoolwork by kerosene lamp.

In spite of what seem like hardships today, when Consumers Power extended one of its lines seven miles to bring electricity to 33 south-central Michigan farms in 1927, initially there were few takers. Consumers Power had assumed the cost of building the Mason-Dansville line itself, and it charged anyone who agreed to wire their farms $3 monthly, plus 5 cents per kilowatt-hour for the first 30

kWh and 3 cents for each additional kWh of electricity they used. Only a dozen families signed up, but it wasn't long before those enthusiastic early adopters convinced others.

"Electricity was the cheapest hired man who ever worked for us," Gerald Thelen, whose family farmed in Fowler, north of Lansing, said in a 1996 survey of Michigan farm families. Instead of spending hours pumping water by hand, he and his family found electricity could do the same job for 31 cents a month. A milking machine could milk 20 cows per hour for one cent; it took two hours to hand-milk the same herd.

By 1937, Consumers Power had more than 10,000 miles of rural lines and 41,307 farm customers. In 1946, a master's degree student at Michigan State University, Richard Schroeder, calculated in his thesis that electric conveniences had saved Michigan farmers more than 50,000 hours of labor in the

When Consumers Power brought traveling displays of electrical wonders to farm communities in the 1920s, women often gathered around trailers demonstrating electric washing machines, promoted here as follows: "Hot and cold water conveyed to tubs through same hose. Tubs emptied through hose attached to bottom … One kilowatt hour current runs washing machine 3 hrs." Meanwhile, men were typically drawn to the Farm Electrification Demonstration Truck, which showed the workings of an automatic light switch, a burglar alarm and a milking machine.

previous 19 years. By 1950, Consumers Power had electrified more than 100,000 farms—more than any other utility in the country.

Although their numbers have declined in recent years, Michigan still has 52,000 farms, and the commodities they produce—corn, dairy, soybeans, livestock, wheat and potatoes, mostly—account for $13 billion of the state's $320 billion economy. Consumers Energy serves more than 30,000 of those farms, more than any other utility in Michigan. The company also sponsors programs that foster pride and longevity in family-farm ownership, train future leaders in farming, and help people commercialize ideas and inventions that might benefit the industry and perpetuate a farming way of life.

Since 1995, the company has contributed more than $300,000 to the Michigan Future Farmers of America to support youth leadership. The company is also active in the Michigan Centennial Farm Association and the Michigan Agricultural Electric Council, sponsoring signs to help customers in its territory honor longtime family farms. There are about 7,000 certified centennial farms in Michigan, the oldest dating back to 1776. In 2015, Consumers Energy awarded 33 Centennial and Sesquicentennial Farm signs to properties that have been farmed by the same family for 100 and 150 years, respectively.

In 2014, Consumers Energy contributed funds to expand the Great Lakes Ag-Tech Business Incubator. The nonprofit initiative jump-starts agricultural innovation by helping farmers and agriculture-related entrepreneurs turn ideas for machines, equipment, software and other inventions into profit-generating assets or new businesses.

As Garrick Rochow, Consumers Energy's senior vice president of distribution and customer operations, said when the business-incubation project was announced, "A strong agricultural industry is vital to Michigan's economic success."

To be designated a Michigan Centennial Farm, below left and right, a property must be a working farm of 10 or more acres continuously owned by the same family for at least 100 years. Consumers Energy donates $20,000 annually to the program.

Big Rock Point employees, below, exit the containment sphere's air lock, one of the plant's many safety features, which ensured that the reactor vessel was in an air-tight environment.

"It was a major upgrade to meet those standards," says Don Baker, then the environmental lead for the Whiting plant. "We installed what are called LO NOx burners, which emit less nitrous oxide, into boilers that really weren't designed for those burners. It took a lot of modifications to the boiler and the pulverizers and the fans, but in the end it worked very well." NOx emissions were reduced by 70 percent, he said.

"GOODBYE, BIG ROCK"
The company spent the entire decade of the 1990s winding down its nuclear operations.

Big Rock Point, a treasured community asset in Charlevoix since 1962 that employed up to 220 local residents, had regularly set operating records:

• Generating a site-record 516,209 megawatt-hours in 1995;

• Operating for more than 23 years, from 1977 to 2000, without a single day of work missed due to injury;

• Beating the world boiling-water reactor record in 1977 by operating for 343 consecutive days.

But time had caught up with Big Rock, and

its operating license was set to expire in May 2000.

"Big Rock Point, as a small, 67-megawatt plant, would have to stand on its own as far as the economics of generating electricity," says Tim Petrosky, Big Rock's public affairs director at the time. "To make the necessary infrastructure enhancements to meet all the regulations going forward would have made the plant uneconomical. Our goal had been for the plant to be the first operating nuclear plant to make it to the end of its license, but the changing economics meant that wasn't going to happen."

On Aug. 29, 1997—35 years to the day after the plant went online—about 1,000 people gathered in the parking lot to watch the scene from the control room on large video screens. With Lee Hausler, the plant manager who had taken the plant critical on its first day in 1962 inside the control room, nuclear control operator Andy Loe pressed the shutdown button.

"Goodbye, Big Rock," he said. "Sorry to see you go."

With that, nine years of safe decommissioning work began to turn Big Rock Point back into a verdant green space, free for unrestricted use by new generations of Michigan residents. The work was exhaustive, meticulous and innovative, made all the more remarkable because Big Rock was one of the first plants in the United States to begin full-scale decommissioning.

Before Consumers Energy could dismantle the plant, it had to decontaminate areas that had been exposed to radiation. Big Rock was the first nuclear plant in the world to use a process called Decontamination for Decommissioning, which uses fluoroboric acid to dissolve contamination. The process, which removed about 90 percent of the contamination in the plant's reactor vessel, earned Consumers Energy and its vendors an R&D 100 award from *R&D Magazine* as one of the most significant technology developments of 1998.

At one point, an army of nearly 500 workers was on site as Big Rock was slowly dismantled; they had undergone hundreds of hours of intensive safety training for nuclear sites.

As part of the decommissioning process, 440 spent nuclear fuel bundles were transferred from the plant's spent-fuel storage pool into large steel and heavily reinforced concrete casks designed to withstand floods, fires, flying objects and tornado winds of up to 360 miles per hour.

Finally, in February 1999, the control room was closed after being staffed 24 hours a day, seven days a week, for more than 37 years. In 2000, the Big Rock Point Restoration Project was named "Project of the Year" by *Power Engineering* magazine. The publication praised the project's system that kept electricity flowing to critical equipment throughout the decommissioning process, as a model of safety and efficiency. The decommissioning process was completed in 2005, with the U.S. Nuclear Regulatory Commission releasing the site for unrestricted use.

CLOSING OUT THE NUCLEAR ERA

The shutdown of Big Rock Point left Palisades as Consumers Energy's sole nuclear plant.

In 1990, Dave Joos had been assigned the task of improving the performance of the struggling Palisades plant, where the average refueling outage lasted three to four months—twice as long as for other plants its size.

As Joos took on the responsibility, Palisades' problems included slow-growing corrosion of tubes that held pressurized water for the plant's two steam generators. Cracks in the tubes posed a risk of contamination, and ultimately the steam generators had to be replaced at great cost—financially and in the form of another extended shutdown beginning in September 1990.

Joos and his team replaced the generators and got the plant back online the following March, but it wasn't long before new problems arose: first, "embrittled" reactor vessel walls that were susceptible to fractures, then a broken fuel rod, then leaking pipes and valves. The plant was shut down for another five months. Nuclear Regulatory Commission fines against the company for violations at Palisades totaled $275,000 between 1992 and 1994 alone.

In the wake of such chronic difficulty, it became clear the company needed to either find a way to operate Palisades differently or sell it. Says Joos, "With only a single nuclear plant, we didn't have the economies of scale that you need. The rest of the company looked at Palisades as an asset that used up resources, the prima donna of the company."

In 2000, Consumers Energy joined the Nuclear Management Company (NMC), an independent nuclear plant operator founded the previous year by four upper Midwest utilities with small nuclear portfolios. NMC, which at its peak operated six Midwest nuclear plants, ran

Cranes lowered tools and supplies and lifted away pieces of the plant, as Big Rock Point was decommissioned and dismantled.

During the final shutdown on Aug. 29, 1997, plant nuclear control operator Andy Loe uttered the memorable words: "Goodbye, Big Rock. Sorry to see you go."

Palisades on behalf of Consumers Energy until 2007, when the company exited the nuclear business altogether by selling the facility to Entergy Nuclear Palisades, LLC.

MICHIGAN DEREGULATES

Outsourcing the management of Palisades allowed CMS Energy to breathe a little more easily, but discontent was simmering on another front. Not everyone at Consumers Energy was happy with the way money was pouring into the unregulated and international businesses, while funds for items such as tree trimming and plant maintenance at the utility were forever short. Those in particular were two areas where Consumers Energy couldn't afford to scrimp—

especially in the competitive retail market that was about to unfold at home, where reliably delivering electricity and providing excellent service at a fair price would mean the difference between keeping a customer and losing one.

"CMS Energy was treating the utility like a cash vehicle," says Phil McAndrews, who joined the company in 1996 as director of investor relations. "At one time, the executives even considered the sale of a 20 percent share of the complete utility, almost like a tracking stock, to raise money to finance all the international operations. Thank goodness that didn't happen."

For decades, the gas and electricity businesses had been highly regulated by the state and federal governments. State public service commissions such as the MPSC oversaw utilities that operated in their states, reviewing investment decisions and authorizing rates paid by customers. The federal government, responding to abusive practices by self-enriching industrialists in the early 20th century, stepped in with the Public Utility Holding Company Act of 1935. Considered one of the most important consumer protection laws ever enacted in the United States, PUHCA limited the activities of utilities' parent companies to prevent owners from charging exorbitant rates, engaging in self-dealing and using customers' money to speculate in questionable ventures. The Securities and Exchange Commission was given the job of enforcing PUHCA and other federal laws pertaining to the energy business.

In return for this regulation, and in recognition of the high cost of building and maintaining power plants and distribution systems, the government granted private companies such as Consumers Energy regional protected territories for the sale of gas and electricity.

Joining the free-market chorus that pervaded government at the time, large commercial and industrial customers began calling for deregulation of retail utility markets in the mid-1990s. They argued that market-based competition—allowing customers to buy power from any company willing and able to sell it to them—would drive down prices. In an odd marriage, environmental organizations backed deregulation as well, believing open-market demand for green power would accelerate the move to renewable energy sources.

New York and California, both of which had sky-high utility rates, were among the first states to adopt deregulated electric markets in the mid-1990s. After a series of public hearings, the Michigan Public Service Commission proposed a framework for restructuring the state's electricity industry, and in June 2000, Gov. John Engler signed the Customer Choice and Electricity Reliability Act. The law affirmed the MPSC's authority to oversee the industry's restructuring, encouraged the commission to foster competition in electricity supply, and gave customers of all of Michigan's investor-owned utilities the right to choose their suppliers as of Jan. 1, 2002.

Michigan's law, like those in other states, separated the discrete functions of supplying (generating), transmitting and delivering electricity, and it allowed competition at the supply and transmission levels of the chain. Local utilities would continue to deliver the power to customers, and in most cases, the utilities were also electricity producers that competed with alternative energy suppliers for the supply contracts.

Anticipating deregulation, Consumers Energy had gotten a jump on customer choice, introducing programs called Gas Customer Choice and Electric Customer Choice in the late 1990s. These guided customers through the process of switching suppliers, and choice programs remain in force today. Regardless of who supplies the energy, Consumers Energy delivers the electricity or gas, reads the meter, performs billing, and responds to outages and service inquiries in its service territory.

Consumers Energy was nimble in preparing itself to respond to deregulation, but it couldn't altogether eliminate the risks. States with full deregulation—including Illinois, New Jersey and Texas—had seen wild price fluctuations along with service-reliability and power-supply problems, and almost none of the rate relief that customers had been promised.

With Michigan's new law cutting residential electric rates by 5 percent and capping them there for four years, there wasn't much competition, as suppliers from out of state hardly clamored for residential customers at unattractive rates. In fact, four years into deregulation, Consumers Energy's residential customers had a choice of only eight alternative energy suppliers besides Consumers Energy; by the end of 2004, those alternative suppliers served just 1,473 customers. The commercial side was another matter, however: competition for the higher-volume business and industrial customers was fierce, and in the first four years of deregulation, Consumers Energy lost at least 950 of those customers. Commercial and industrial sales declined from a total of 1,920,220 megawatt hours in 2001 to 1,726,680 megawatt hours in 2004.

The new law required Michigan's major utilities to either divest their transmission systems or turn operation of the grid over to an independent company. So it was that in October 2001, Consumers Energy announced an agreement to sell its transmission network to a partnership led by Trans-Elect for approximately

The replacement of two steam generators at the Palisades Nuclear Plant in 1992 represented the first removal of a nuclear plant's steam generator in a single lift to save outage time and reduce workers' exposure to radiation.

$290 million. The agreement marked the nation's first sale of a major utility's transmission system to an independent entity. The cash was used to improve Consumers Energy's balance sheet—something that would soon be desperately needed.

TROUBLE OVERSEAS

With the international properties performing well, the uncertainty of the nuclear operations in the rear-view mirror and Consumers Energy better focused on its core utility business, CMS Energy seemed to have nothing but blue skies ahead. The company was riding high—or so it appeared.

Internationally, CMS Energy continued to aggressively expand its holdings in the early 2000s. It already owned Jorf Lasfar, a 1,356-megawatt, coal-fueled plant in Morocco that was the largest independent power facility in Africa and the Middle East. In 2001, Al Taweelah A2, a 710-megawatt power and desalination plant on the Arabian gulf about 50 miles northeast of Abu Dhabi, opened as the first private power project awarded in the United Arab Emirates. The following year, Shuweihat S1, a similar but larger (1,125-megawatt) plant southwest of the city, entered commercial operation; it became the world's largest independent power and water desalination project.

Jewels like these could not compensate for the many unwise investments the company

The problems in Australia and South America were worse.

In Australia, Vic Fryling, CMS Energy president and chief operating officer, had led the purchase of a brown coal-fueled electricity plant called Loy Yang A in Victoria province. The CMS Energy-led consortium that bought Loy Yang and its associated coal mine had paid $3.67 billion in 1997, a jaw-dropping amount that took nearly a dozen banks to finance.

"The company clearly paid too much," says Tom Elward, then head of CMS Energy's domestic and international operations. Shortly after the sale closed, government-owned power plants in New South Wales that weren't driven by profits started competing aggressively with CMS Energy on the open market. Over time, the asset lost value and eventually was worth less than CMS Energy had paid.

"It was ultra-competitive, with bids on power pricing every hour," Elward says. "There were a lot of fixed costs, and you couldn't fix the revenue to compensate. The plant was financed at a 10 percent interest rate, equating to just under one million Australian dollars per day. I used to say, 'Every day I get up, there goes another million dollars in interest at Loy Yang.'"

GOING BACK HOME

The South American enterprise was very successful at first, but a decade after CMS Energy entered Argentina in its first global gambit, the company faced one roadblock after another—a result of the country's chronic political and economic instability.

"Argentina has had an up-and-down record of business friendliness forever," says Dave Joos. "It shifts from socialism to capitalism and back again."

The Atacama pipeline to carry Argentine natural gas into Chile through the driest desert in the world stalled when the government established price controls in an effort to stem years of economic crisis. CMS Energy's construction plans included a $400 million pipeline and, in partnership with an Argentine company, a $500 million natural gas plant; the gas was to power a copper mine in Chile. But the

CMS Energy's 1997 shared purchase of the Loy Yang A coal-fueled plant in Victoria, Australia, didn't turn out as planned. The investment foreshadowed the downfall of the company's international portfolio.

made, however, and bets that CMS Energy made on a number of its overseas ventures started to show fault lines. Trouble surfaced in Turkey, Australia, Argentina and Venezuela.

In 1998, a consortium led by CMS Energy was selected as the exclusive electricity distributor and operator of Turkey's Bursa-Yalova electric distribution systems, with approximately 700,000 customers. But a 7.6 magnitude earthquake in Izmit in 1999 destroyed most of its assets, and CMS Energy never closed on the deal.

"We weren't going to buy and rebuild the utility," Frank Johnson says. "Then the government changed, so we just walked away from that one."

price controls had the effect of restricting gas supplies, and as Joos says, "There wasn't much excess gas, and the pipeline was suddenly not such a good investment."

One of CMS Energy's overseas investments was a privatizing electric utility that served 90,000 customers on Margarita Island, off the shore of Venezuela. A CMS Energy-led coalition bid $63 million for a 70 percent stake in the utility in September 1998. The purchase included a diesel-fired generating plant and an underwater cable connecting the island with the mainland.

"We bought the whole thing—generation, transmission and distribution," says Frank Johnson. "It was the biggest piece of junk I had ever seen in my life."

When Hugo Chavez became Venezuela's president in 1999, he ended privatization of the oil industry, putting the last nail in the coffin of the Margarita Island venture.

"We were the only privatized utility company in the country, and the asset never made a dime," Elward says.

Meanwhile, the U.S. energy market was changing. With the economy slowing and corporate earnings falling, investors demanded the opposite of what they had wanted in the go-go 1990s: strong balance sheets with low debt

levels and low business risk. Glamorous but risky international investments were on the way out, and the predictability of old-fashioned utilities was suddenly in demand again.

It was not a good time for CMS Energy to be juggling a high level of debt and a large portfolio of assets, many of which were producing little or no income. CMS Energy therefore decided to get out of the volatile international business, making plans to sell more than $6 billion in overseas and non-core assets that at one point had contributed about a third of the company's earnings. The sale included the company's international plants, utilities and pipeline interests and the company's non-utility natural gas operations in northern Michigan. Unwinding the international business would take six years.

At the annual meeting in May 2001, the company announced that it would sell its international and other assets and return to "a North American focus." Bill McCormick told shareholders the company expected "a good year this year, and we're very pleased about that." He noted, however, that the debt on the books from all the international purchases still had to be serviced.

ROUND TRIP

As part of its move into unregulated businesses in the 1990s, CMS Energy formed a Houston-based subsidiary—CMS Marketing, Services and Trading—to buy and sell energy futures. It was later learned that, during 2000 and 2001, that subsidiary conducted $4.4 billion in so-called prearranged "round-trip" electricity trades with two other companies, Dynegy and Reliant Resources.

Round-trip trading—defined by the Federal Energy Regulatory Commission as a prearranged pair of trades between the same parties involving no economic risk and no net change in beneficial ownership—was neither illegal nor unique to CMS Energy. It was a common practice known as "pumping up the volume," according to longtime company board member John Yasinsky. He says that while round-trip trading didn't affect earnings or cash flow, it did inflate a company's order

CEO Bill McCormick announced his retirement at the company's 2002 annual shareholders' meeting.

book, making it appear to be "a key player in the energy trading business" and enabling it to report higher revenues.

By the time round-trip practices at CMS Energy came to light in May 2002, Enron had already gone bankrupt under a cloud of suspicious trading and fraudulent accounting, and the revelation shook the confidence of CMS Energy investors—not to mention that of the MPSC. The Securities and Exchange Commission investigated, and CMS Energy acknowledged that the electricity wash trades had inflated its revenue by $5.2 billion in 2000 and 2001, accounting for about 23.3 percent of its revenue in those years.

These issues alone probably wouldn't have threatened CMS Energy's survival, but the problem was compounded when the company's outside auditor, Arthur Andersen—which would later go under in the Enron fallout—refused to certify the company's financial statements unless the company obtained a loan of nearly $1 billion. Without audited financial statements, bank agreements were technically invalid, and it would be nearly impossible for the company to obtain new credit.

Says Phil McAndrews, the company's then-investor relations director, "CMS Energy had not put any equity into the utility for so long because we were going into the international deals. The utility was growing and earning more, but the equity stayed low and the return was exceeding state-authorized levels."

Class-action lawsuits were filed against CMS Energy, alleging that the company had made false and misleading statements about its financial position and committed severe accounting improprieties. CMS Energy stock, which had closed at $20.25 per share on the day the company declared its first-quarter dividend on May 3, 2002, began a free fall, and senior management seriously entertained the possibility of bankruptcy for the second time in 16 years.

"In the mid-1980s, it was almost taboo that a utility would declare bankruptcy," says Carl English, former president and CEO of Consumers Energy's gas operation. "The MPSC wasn't ready then to make Michigan the first state where that happened, but by 2002, the veil had been broken. Utilities in California and New Hampshire had filed for bankruptcy. We thought it could really happen this time."

By May 24, the night before the 2002 annual meeting at the Dearborn Inn—with CMS Energy's shares trading at $17.63—the board of directors met privately over dinner to discuss the company's precarious position. One by one, they inventoried the negatives: Bad investments overseas. A plummeting stock price. The refusal of auditors to certify its financial statements. Demands from the MPSC for a rate decrease based on the potentially deceptive revenue statements. A raft of pending lawsuits. And, of course, the round-trip electricity trades themselves. Together, they added up to a clear message: Consumers Energy was on the rocks, and it couldn't be steered to clear water by the man who had navigated the company into the torrent in the first place.

The next morning, the annual meeting began in an atmosphere markedly different from those of recent years past, when elaborate videos had highlighted investments in South America, India, the Middle East and Australia. With no backdrop, a somber McCormick took the stage and announced his retirement.

The assembled shareholders—many of them retirees of the utility who lived locally—broke into spontaneous applause. For years, they had watched as money generated by their beloved utility was sucked into international businesses and as the utility became starved of investment, its performance, along with their reward for hard work and loyalty, declining.

"People weren't happy," English says. "Trees weren't getting trimmed, gas lines were not being maintained well, there were increasing outages. There had been tremendous frustration throughout the company, and those local shareholders really felt it personally."

As the applause died down and as enthusiasm and relief gave way to reality, people in the crowd began looking at one another, the same question at the top of their minds: Who is going to lead us out of this mess?

The company started a comeback in the 2000s by returning to its core utility business.

6: From the Brink

Former automotive executive Ken Whipple took the helm of Consumers Energy during one of the most challenging times in the company's history.

K

en Whipple wasn't a utility man. Though he had served on the board of CMS Energy since 1993, he was really a car guy, having spent 40 years with Ford Motor Co., including positions as president of Ford Financial Services and CEO of Ford Motor Credit. He retired as a full-time executive in 1999, but his retirement didn't last long.

Immediately after Bill McCormick resigned as president and CEO in May 2002, the CMS Energy Board of Directors voted unanimously to name a new leader to step onto the bridge and right the course: Ken Whipple. It didn't matter that he didn't know the finer points of the energy business. He knew enough from nine years as an outside board member—and what mattered most, anyway, was his leadership skill at a time when Consumers Energy desperately needed it.

Today, Whipple jokes that "I got the short straw," but he says that at the time, "it was intriguing, an entirely different kind of challenge."

Accepting the monumental task of restoring CMS Energy and Consumers Energy to health, Whipple stood in a jammed auditorium in Consumers Energy's main building on Michigan Avenue in Jackson, where anxious employees were gathered to hear his plan to save their company. Whipple was a plain-spoken, straightforward man, and his message was so simple it could be summed up in three words: back to basics. CMS Energy would move aggressively ahead with the North American strategy that McCormick had announced the previous year and make it the sole focus of the company.

"We will do the things we know how to do well," Whipple announced. "We know how to build and run power plants, and we know how to transport raw materials and power products within our geographic area. We have a strong, well-operated gas and electric utility that's the backbone of the company, and that's not going to change."

The glamour days were over.

"ARE WE OKAY NOW?"

Under the plan formulated by Whipple and the board, CMS Energy would reduce its aspirations for high growth and concentrate instead on running a well-performing utility and paying down debt. Especially important were being realistic about growth, achieving financial targets and behaving with unimpeachable integrity.

"If we say we're going to meet $1.75 earnings per share, we'd better meet $1.75," Whipple said. "Ethics and integrity? They only come in doses of 100 percent."

To bring costs in line, restore the confidence of investors, employees and customers and keep a focus on the basics, CMS Energy embarked on an austerity program—starting at the top. Whipple would defer his own compensation and base it on stock performance. The company would close its Dearborn headquarters and combine it with Consumers Energy's Jackson headquarters and reduce the workforce by 50 employees. Offices in Houston and London would be closed. The company's 401(k) retirement-program match for employees

Consumers Energy's back-to-basics strategy refocused the company on doing what it did best: serving the people of Michigan.

Recruited from Kellogg by Ken Whipple, Chief Financial Officer Tom Webb played a key role in returning the company to financial health.

would be suspended for 28 months. The corporate jets would be sold.

"Here's this Michigan utility that owns four Falcon-900s, the same kind of corporate plane Ford had," Whipple says. "Sure, they made it easier to get to some hard-to-access places, but when you're asking people to forego contributions to their 401(k), that one was an easy decision to make. You just have to ask yourself, 'What are you doing that seems dumb?' and then stop doing that."

Whipple went on a barnstorming tour through Consumers Energy's regional offices with a message that was blunt but, to employees, reassuring. As he settled into his role and dug deeply into the company's inner workings, however, he realized the true scope of the challenge he'd undertaken and how much tougher it would be to convince outsiders—especially Wall Street—that a renaissance was in the making.

Whipple told investors the company was

committed to continual year-over-year earnings growth, but delivering on that promise wouldn't be easy. Consumers Energy had hired Ernst & Young to replace Arthur Andersen, and, as Whipple recounts, the auditors' opinion was not good: "We didn't have enough funds to operate for a couple of years. The new auditors were very close to declaring us insolvent."

Whipple had built up goodwill on Wall Street during his time as the head of Ford Credit, so he paid visits to "every bank in New York," trying to line up sources of liquidity. "We came back from New York with $2 billion in credit, a few days away from insolvency, and said, 'Are we okay now?'" The answer was a resounding "hardly."

"IN MORE TROUBLE THAN YOU THINK"

The infusion was only a stopgap, and the company remained in free fall. Whipple knew that it would take years to restore CMS Energy to fiscal health and that if the effort were going to succeed, he would need a trusted financial genius by his side. He placed a call to a former colleague, Thomas Webb, and invited him to dinner. Webb and Whipple had worked in Ford's European division together in the 1980s. As chief financial officer at Kellogg Company, Webb had just helped that company in a major turnaround achieve its best cash flow in history.

"I had no idea what CMS Energy or Consumers Energy were until the summer of 2002 when Ken and I met for dinner," says Webb. "I checked the Internet and realized what was happening. He was looking for a CFO. We sat down to dinner, and I offered names. He smiled and said, 'I don't need names. I want you.'"

Webb told Whipple there were two problems.

"The first is that I don't know anything about your business except that we're customers, and my wife, who pays the bills, says you charge too much," Webb said.

"Don't worry," Whipple replied. "Where we're different, it's easy to learn, and where we're not, that's where I need your help. I need someone I can trust as my number one in getting us out of this financial debacle. Now, what's the second problem?"

"I think you're in a lot more trouble than you

think you're in," Webb said. "When you're in real trouble and people have lost faith, they all think about you as certain to fail. They're no longer trying to help you. They're trying to minimize their own risk."

Based largely on his respect for and trust in Whipple, Webb began work as executive vice president and chief financial officer of CMS Energy and Consumers Energy during the summer of 2002. He barely had time to find a parking space before Whipple summoned him and Dave Joos, then president and chief operating officer of CMS Energy, to a meeting.

"I walked in the door to see five gloomy faces around a big round table," Webb says. "This was clearly not a welcome party."

Whipple explained that one of the company's creditors was demanding several hundred million dollars in collateral immediately, triggered by credit downgrades.

"Do they have the right to it?" Webb asked.

"They do," replied Whipple.

"Do we have the money?" Webb asked. The answer was no.

"Who's working on this?" was Webb's last inquiry.

"You," said Whipple. "It just came up last week, and we didn't want to tell you before you got here."

Webb promptly flew to New York, accompanied by one company lawyer, to sit across a table facing about a dozen or so of the creditor's attorneys.

"It appears you have the right to get your money," Webb told them. "But there's a fair chance it'll put us into bankruptcy. I looked at the list of who gets paid first if that happens, and you're pretty far down the list, so if you put us into bankruptcy, you won't get your money." He then hummed a few bars of the Rolling Stones' song "You Can't Always Get What You Want."

The company sold its 5,400-mile transmission system in 2001 as part of a back-to-basics strategy.

The TriMars compressor station in the Gulf of Mexico was part of the Trunkline distribution system that brought gas from the Gulf Coast north to Consumers Power customers, via 11,500 miles of mainline gas pipe. Opposite, the company received additional natural gas supply at the Indiana border near White Pigeon, Mich., from the Trunkline Gas Co. in 1960. Pictured, from left, at the valve-turning ceremony are then-Michigan Gov. G. Mennen Williams, Trunkline President W.K. Sanders and Al Aymond, chairman of the Consumers Power Board of Directors. The company sold these Trunkline assets in 2002.

No one on the other side of the table laughed.

"Not even a smile," Webb recalls, chuckling. "But I said, 'All I can do is tell you that's where we are. You have the choice to force it, but if you have someone on the business side who'd like to work with us, we're willing to.'"

By the time Webb returned to Michigan, the creditor's CEO had called Ken Whipple to complain. But the creditor backed off its demand for the additional money, and that crisis was averted.

NARROWING THE FOCUS

With the worst of the immediate bleeding staunched, it was time to begin the real surgery. Webb and Tom Elward, by that time CMS Enterprises president and chief operating officer, began selling off CMS Energy's non-core assets.

While the majority of the operations sold were international, probably the most painful divestiture was a domestic one: CMS Panhandle companies, which comprised the Panhandle-

Trunkline gas pipeline system the company had purchased for $2.2 billion in 1998. CMS Energy sold the Panhandle companies to Southern Union Panhandle Corp. in December 2002, taking a $700 million loss. Analysts commended the company for making a commitment to strengthen its balance sheet.

"[CMS Energy is] taking a clear path to financial security," Timothy O'Brien, who managed more than a half-million shares of CMS Energy stock in the Evergreen Utility and Telecommunications Fund, told the *Detroit News*. "If they sell assets and pay down debt, the result is [a company] that's solidly investment grade."

On the international side, the company sold 15 assets in 2003, the sales of $2.1 billion garnering net proceeds of $850 million.

"We took a lot of losses," says Phil McAndrews, investor relations director at the time. "Morocco was a jewel, probably one of the best assets we owned, and then our oil and gas operations were very profitable. We sold part of those to Marathon for $1 billion, including some

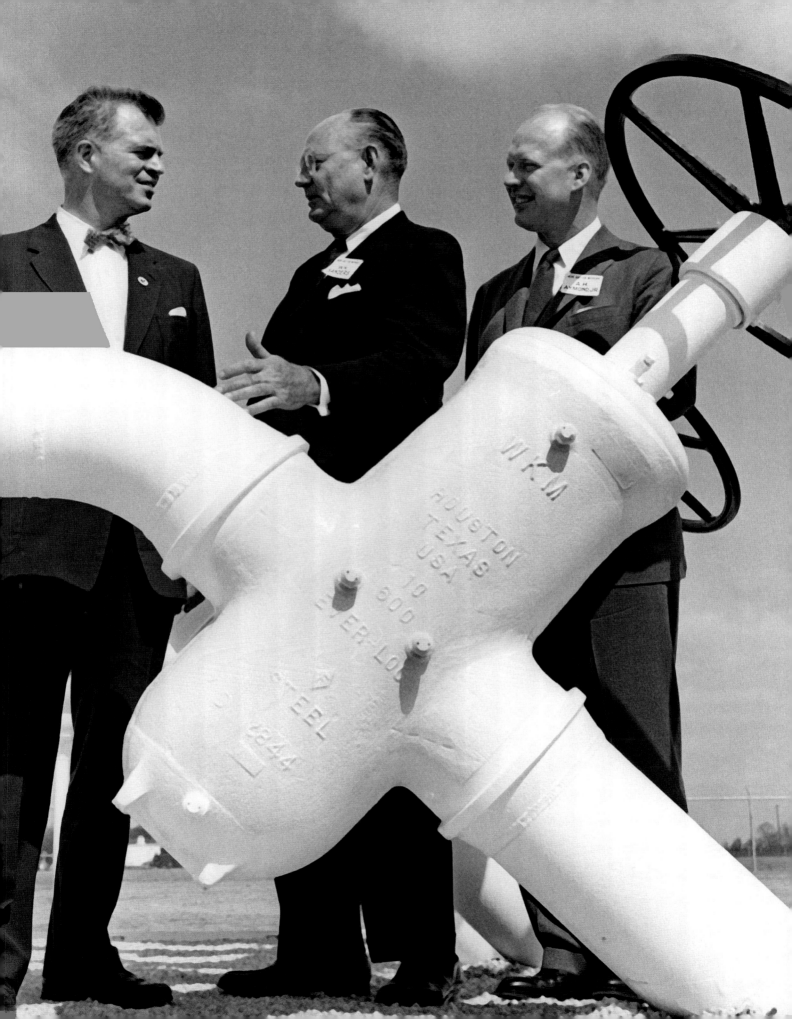

Jorf Lasfar in Morocco was one of the last international assets sold, helping to put the company on better financial footing—as CEO Ken Whipple was able to show employees and shareholders, opposite, in 2004.

terrific assets in Equatorial Guinea. Practically everything in South America sold at a loss."

The sales and the austerity program began to achieve their desired effect. CMS Energy still had to ride its stock to the bottom—on March 11, 2003, it closed at $3.49 a share—as investors' confidence built that a sustainable rebound was under way.

"There was no stopping it," says Tom Webb. "We just had to hang on."

In April 2003, Whipple announced that the company at last had "real, final, audited financial statements" for the previous three years and had secured $1.4 billion in new financing to cover maturities at CMS Energy and Consumers Energy well into 2004. At around the same time, Moody's Investor Services upgraded its ratings outlook from "review for possible downgrade" to "stable" for both CMS Energy and Consumers Energy on the strength of the company's asset sales, debt reduction, improved liquidity, suspension of the common stock dividend, completion of the re-audits and the continuing sound performance of the utility.

By the end of 2003, Whipple was able to write a letter for the annual report that began, in his typical straightforward tone: "Dear Shareholders: 2003 was a lot better year than 2002 for your company. Maybe that's not saying much, as 2002 was a pretty lousy benchmark, and we didn't hit all home runs last year, but the place is clearly on the mend. The way we put it with our employees is that we're out of intensive care. We're not ready to run marathons yet, but we're well into rehab."

CMS Energy had reduced its debt by $2.1 billion, or 25 percent, since 2001 to stand at $6.2 billion at the end of 2003. By the end of 2004, earnings were positive for the first time in several years: net income was $110 million, or 64 cents per share, compared with a loss of $44 million, or 30 cents per share, in the previous year.

COUNT ON US—AGAIN

According to board member John Yasinsky, the ability of Whipple, Joos and Webb to steer CMS Energy onto a clear course, to set and

communicate realistic goals and to repeatedly achieve them injected a positive attitude and refreshed the company's can-do culture almost immediately.

"The most important driver became commitment to continuous improvement and establishing objectives that were consistently met," Yasinsky says. "It helped to establish trust again: from our customers, our employees and our shareholders."

When it came time to negotiate a labor contract for the Consumers Energy call center, which had voted to unionize in 2002, it became clear to employees how much things had changed.

"We were at loggerheads on a couple of issues," recalls Steve Van Slooten, then a statewide union representative. "I requested a meeting with Ken Whipple, and to my amazement he agreed to meet with me directly. With his guidance, we were able to come to an agreement. He was able to listen to both sides and make a decision that was in the best interests of everybody."

Complementing the strategy to rid itself of esoteric, non-core operations and clean up its balance sheet was perhaps the most important work of all: making sure the people of Michigan had reliable, affordable power. Accordingly, Consumers Energy boosted its investments in customer service and system maintenance.

"We had skimped on reliability investment for a while, partly because of liquidity concerns, and neglected our infrastructure," Whipple says. "That's an easy way to cut costs: just don't trim the trees. But it comes back to bite you when the wind comes up and the trees hit power lines, and you have to do an emergency fix. We brought that investment back up to about $45 million annually on line-clearing work alone."

Consumers Energy had regained its true north—and from 2003 on, the company never broke its commitments to deliver earnings growth every year and to reinvest continually in the reliability of its infrastructure.

When the blackout of August 2003 hit, Consumers Energy was ready. Although the system lost about 2,500 megawatts of

2003: A Turnaround Year — Liquidity Peace

- 81¢ a share
- Cash flow improved
- Debt reduced $1.1 billion
- $3.6 billion refinanced
- Capital and cost efficiencies achieved
- $560 million paid into pension fund

CMS Debt (Billions)

$8.3

$7.3

$6.9
6.2

Accounting Change

$6.5
5.8

2001   2002   2003   2004

"The way we put it with our employees is that we're out of intensive care. We're not ready to run marathons yet, but we're well into rehab."

Keeping it Clean

One of the many non-utility investments CMS Energy made through the subsidiaries of CMS Land and CMS Capital in the 1990s was a loan to the developer of a luxury real estate development near the city of Petoskey, on the shores of Little Traverse Bay—a loan that gave the company the right to serve the property and its thousands of potential new customers with electricity. The idea was to turn the former site of a cement plant into the "ultimate lifestyle resort."

When the developer died with the loan unpaid, the property now known as Bay Harbor fell into CMS Land Company's hands. In 1994, the company teamed with another developer, David Johnson, to bring the resort's plans to fruition. The completed resort boasted a deepwater marina, yacht club, equestrian center, golf course and residential neighborhoods full of multi-million-dollar homes. Bay Harbor still sparkles

above Lake Michigan, a destination that one Yelp reviewer called "speechless, hands down, I-see-God-beautiful."

CMS Land Company has had no ownership in the property for more than a decade. As the company divested itself of non-utility assets in the dark days of 2002, Bay Harbor became one of the first properties to go—but CMS Land Company agreed to retain legal liability for any environmental issues. That liability turned out to be costly, because Bay Harbor's golf course had been built on kiln dust from the cement plant. Michigan's environmental regulators had approved a plan to stabilize the dust by incorporating it into the development. In addition, CMS Land Company agreed to collect runoff, called leachate, from the dust that was high in alkalinity and mercury and contained traces of arsenic and other metals left in the soil from the cement plant's days; the runoff

A roller worked the cap as part of the final remedy in the Bay Harbor remediation, above. Water entering the cleanup plants could exceed 60 parts per trillion of mercury; coming out, it ranged between .5 parts per trillion to 1.5 parts per trillion.

would be diverted to a wastewater treatment plant in Petoskey.

In 2004, elevated alkaline levels were identified in shoreline waters near each of the kiln dust piles. Heavy metals, including mercury and vanadium, were also found at levels exceeding Michigan's water quality standards.

"The contaminated runoff was seeping into the lake long before Bay Harbor was built," says CMS Land's Michael Sniegowski, the vice president and executive project manager who oversaw the project. "The original development and remediation plan dramatically improved and protected the environment and turned an abandoned moonscape into a world-class destination."

Although the newly identified environmental issues were not CMS Energy's fault, CMS Land Company accepted the legal liability and was committed to cleaning it up—

even though it cost the company more than $315 million above what it had initially paid to remediate environmental issues at the site. Initially, CMS Land collected and shipped leachate to a deep injection well about 60 miles from the site. Sniegowski estimates CMS Land trucked between 150,000 and 300,000 gallons of neutralized water every day from 2006 through 2011. Ultimately, the company built two water treatment plants to treat the collected water on site before releasing it into the bay.

Sniegowski says: "This decade-long environmental effort at Bay Harbor and adjoining East Park have provided environmental protection few other sites can match. This once-abandoned site has been returned to productive use and continues to draw visitors from around the world while providing economic benefit to Northern Michigan."

An aerial view, below, shows the Bay Harbor community. After many years of monitoring verified the effectiveness of the remedies, the Health Department of Northern Michigan lifted its last remaining health advisory at Bay Harbor.

generating capacity—more than a third of its supply—in an instant, Ludington, the company's baseload coal generation plants and Palisades nuclear plant helped to keep the grid from collapsing. Employees at Karn-Weadock, Campbell, Cobb and Whiting worked overnight and returned from vacations to restore power, while retirees and off-duty supervisors and operators volunteered as well. Less than 24 hours after the blackout started, power was restored to all of Consumers Energy's customers.

In the eyes of many customers, they had their "good old Consumers Energy" back.

PASSING THE TORCH

By 2004, Whipple, hired as an interim leader, felt that he had done what he set out to do: put CMS Energy and Consumers Energy back on course.

"I might have liked to stay a little longer," he says. "Things were looking up, and it was a lot of fun to come to work. But we clearly had the next CEO in the house and ready to go in the person of Dave Joos. It was his turn to lead and the right time to do it."

Whipple returned to the board of directors, as chairman, and Joos took up the CEO's mantle. Joos had been a figure of leadership

at Consumers Energy for nearly 30 years, an imposing figure of 6-foot-3 who had arrived for his first day of work at Big Rock Point in 1976 wearing platform shoes and bell bottoms. He was trusted at every level of the company. His mantra, a variation of Whipple's back to basics, was that it was time to *build* on the basics: "We need to make major investments in pipeline safety, clean air and distribution reliability," he said.

With Consumers Energy's costs under control, debt at its lowest levels in more than three years and the company's performance on the upswing across the board, Joos was able to reach into the capital markets to make those investments. The company raised $560 million in new equity through the sale of CMS Energy common stock, and it plowed $800 million into Consumers Energy.

By 2005, the stock price had jumped 60 percent over the previous year, and employees saw the return of the company match to their retirement savings plan. Moreover, after 10 years in which the utility's base rates had been frozen—except for a 5 percent rate cut in 2000—Consumers Energy filed for a rate increase of $320 million.

Dave Joos, named CEO of CMS Energy and Consumers Energy in 2004, met with reporters in 2007 to announce an 830-megawatt "clean coal" plant near Bay City. Ultimately, construction of the plant was canceled in 2011 because of market factors such as reduced demand for electricity, surplus generating capacity in the Midwest market and lower natural gas prices.

"If our rates had increased at the same rate as the Consumer Price Index, residential customers would be paying 10 cents per kilowatt hour today, instead of the current rate of 8 cents," Ronn Rasmussen, the company's executive director of rates and group controller, said in an interview at the time. "We're serving more customers with more electricity, and our generating plants are running at record levels. We need a rate increase to continue to provide safe, reliable and responsive electric service."

The MPSC, now convinced that the company was placing its Michigan customers' interests first, approved the request.

BIG ROCK: THE FINAL CHAPTER

On Aug. 29, 2006, the 44th anniversary of the licensure of the Big Rock Point nuclear plant, a celebration marked the site's full transformation into a greenfield. Attendees scattered grass seed along mulch paths in the plant's old footprint, and children played in the soil where the reactor building once stood.

Among the speakers at the celebration was Odawa tribal chairman Frank Ettawageshik, whose ancestors had used the big rock on the nearby Lake Michigan shore as a navigational aid and meeting place for hundreds of years. He said the plant had completed its circle of life.

"The big rock was a landmark for our people," he said. "Although this is an ending, this is also a beginning. This was a place of service for jobs and energy. Today is a transition. This is a time when this land will remain in service as a group of us are working to retain this land in a way that will be useful for future generations."

Dave Joos, who had started his career at Big Rock, watched the celebration with pride.

"I wondered how difficult it was going to be for people to work on tearing something down that they had spent so many years putting their hearts and souls into," he said. "I guess I shouldn't have been surprised that folks took every bit as much pride in doing that job right from the beginning. They will leave a legacy here that will be long remembered—not just by the people locally but by the whole nuclear community—that this is how you do it."

Today, on a walk around the grounds where the reactor once sat, there's no indication of what was there but for a monument created by former employees calling themselves the Big Rock Historical Society. They raised close to $1 million for the marker along Big Rock Drive, made from pieces of steel from the containment unit. Diagrams and images tell the stories: of the plant itself on one side and of the Odawa tribal nation and the big rock that gave the plant its name on the other.

Consumers Energy still owns the 435 acres surrounding Big Rock Point. While no decisions have yet been made about its future, the company intends to keep it in its restored natural state.

CONCERNS IN A VOLATILE MARKET

For the first century of the company's history, the domestic energy market was relatively stable, but the changes that stacked atop one another through the later decades of the 20th century created increasingly volatile markets and unpredictable business conditions. By the early 2000s, dramatic fluctuations in energy prices and availability, environmental challenges and the burden of ever tougher regulations

The Big Rock Point nuclear plant site was fully converted to a greenfield by 2006.

Safety Success

There was a time when the culture at Consumers Energy and, indeed, throughout the industry, was to keep a power plant running at all times, virtually at all costs.

Richard Ford recalls an incident in which wet coal got stuck in pipes when he was site manager at Consumers Energy's Karn-Weadock coal-fired facility in the mid-2000s. Employees tried to loosen the wet coal by pounding on the coal pipes and using metal bars inserted into the coal feeders.

When supervisors told employees that that was dangerous and that the plant should be taken down for cleaning, employees resisted in order to keep the plant's operational time as high as possible. Acknowledging the employees' good intentions, Ford ordered the plant shut down so the pipes could be vacuumed out safely while the unit wasn't running.

"It used to be that you kept the unit on, no matter what," says Ford. "A lot of people had come up in that mind-set, and our safety record was declining. We had to get on a path to improvement."

The transformation of the safety culture at Consumers Energy began with an unprecedented "safety summit" in May 2005 involving company executives and the presidents of 14 utility workers' union locals from around the state. The daylong workshop was led by experts in organizational behavior who had helped companies including General Motors and Public Service Electric & Gas create participatory safety cultures.

The summit "opened our eyes to things that were pretty obvious but have been overlooked," Paul Preketees, senior vice president of gas operations, told the company newsletter at the time. "We still need to get customers back online and respond to their emergencies in a timely manner. We still need to generate and deliver reliable electricity, and we still need to strive to be the utility that customers value. But we will do it with the mind-set that safety comes first."

Of course, nearly every company says safety comes first—but at the time, Consumers Energy couldn't demonstrate that.

"There were trucks out in the field at night with no reflective stickers on the doors, employees out in the field not wearing personal protective equipment and taking shortcuts, putting themselves at risk to get

Consumers Energy adopted the National Incident Management System (NIMS), developed by the Department of Homeland Security, as a new company-wide standard to further align with police, fire and other first responders during electric and natural gas emergencies.

After a 2005 Safety Summit, Consumers Energy formed a companywide Safety Culture Transition Team, which in turn created 31 local teams responsible for addressing safety concerns in their areas of responsibility. The dramatic results of those efforts can be seen in the chart below.

the job done," says Dan Malone, senior vice president of energy resources.

The essence of Consumers Energy's safety program is captured by the slogan "Stop the Job." If something isn't right, every employee has the right to stop the job, no matter where he or she is or what the issue is.

"We're not going to proceed if it's unsafe," says Malone, who made himself a constant presence in the field, showing up at job sites to assess safety measures. "I'd get to the first site of the day, and no one would be wearing protective gear or using safety cones. By the third site, they'd have every cone known to man out there and all the safety gear on. It didn't take long for word to get out: Malone's in the field."

Notwithstanding the improvement in safety that came, at least anecdotally, from a greater awareness of safety and a realization that leadership was watching, some senior executives were skeptical when, in 2007, John Russell, then president and chief operating officer of Consumers Energy, called for a 50 percent reduction in on-the-job accidents within five years.

"They told me: 'You don't understand, this is a dangerous business,'" Russell says. "I said, 'That's the goal. If you can't work safe, you can't work for us.'"

Consumers Energy didn't meet the goal in five years; it achieved it in two. So Russell upped the ante: reduce reportable safety incidents by 70 percent before the five years are out. At the end of five years, in 2012, incidents were down more than 78 percent,

and 2016 represented the safest year in company history.

In 2014, Consumers Energy created four full-time permanent positions—one management and three union—dedicated to improving the company's safety culture. One of the employees suggested that the company hire athletic trainers. Today, there are 19 trainers to educate employees about wellness, nutrition and fitness; evaluate and treat pains, sprains and strains; and help make work stations and daily jobs healthier. The theory is that physically fit workers are less likely to have accidents and better able to handle a situation if it occurs.

"You might say that's expensive, but since we started this program, we've cut about $25 million annually in worker's compensation costs, so it's more than paid for itself while making sure we become a safer, more productive utility," Malone says.

For many Consumers Energy employees, safety is personal. In June 2012, journeyman lineworker Jeffery Creel, a father of four, was struck by an automobile and killed on his last storm restoration job of the day.

"He had his vest on, he was putting his cones and signs out, and a passing vehicle swerved and hit him," Malone says. "He was doing everything right—but a lot of employees weren't, and when they lost one of their own, it really brought it home to them."

In response, Consumers Energy spent $5 million to outfit its field vehicles with special warning lights, and Creel's colleagues created a campaign in his memory: Correct RoadsidE ProtEction Saves Lives (CREEL). Window decals placed on company trucks bear the campaign name, show the company and union logos, and remind workers to be careful.

"They're the last thing you see as you exit your truck," says Malone.

Steve Van Slooten, a Consumers Energy plant mechanic who serves as national vice president of the Utility Workers' Union of America, AFL-CIO, says that while there will always be disagreements between the company and the union, "one thing we always agree on is that we want to have the highest-skilled, safest workplace in the world."

EMPLOYEE SAFETY
Recordable Incidents

Year	Incidents
2005	562
2006	495
2007	558
2008	355
2009	258
2010	207
2011	160
2012	119
2013	137
2014	150
2015	106
2016	73

While Consumers Energy played an active role in Michigan's debate over electricity regulation, its main focus remained on providing the best service to customers.

became daily challenges in the energy industry. The constant change and uncertainty placed enormous pressure on utilities such as Consumers Energy.

One of the great areas of uncertainty stemmed from the state's experiment with electric deregulation in 2000. The underlying theory was a deregulated market would create widespread competition, lower prices for customers, and encourage independent energy companies to invest in new power plants.

Reality was far different. Instead of widespread competition, the alternative energy suppliers, mainly out-of-state power marketers, focused on the high-volume customers. Not a single residential customer on Consumers Energy's system was ever served by an alternate supplier.

While a relative handful of the state's customers, mainly large businesses, benefited, the overwhelming majority of customers ended up paying higher bills, because more of the utilities' fixed costs were shifted to them.

Meanwhile, although the customer demand for electricity was rising steadily, no independent company stepped forward to build a new baseload power plant.

The major utilities found Michigan's deregulation approach created too much uncertainty for them to obtain reasonable financing for major projects needed to serve customers, despite the growing need for substantial investments in the state's energy infrastructure.

The main problem with Michigan's hybrid deregulation: Customers could buy their power from an alternative energy supplier when prices on the open market were low and come back to the utilities' regulated rates when market prices rose.

Plus, the law required utilities to take back customers. It also required them to provide power to customers being served by alternative energy suppliers if the suppliers couldn't provide the electricity their customers needed.

Under this system, utilities didn't know how many customers they would have from day to day or how much power they'd have to be ready to supply to their customers.

The fluctuations were large and came quickly. Between 2003 and 2006, 3,000 megawatts of the state's electricity load—roughly the amount generated by three large baseload plants—went to the alternative energy suppliers and then back to the utilities.

The 21st Century Electric Energy Plan, an independent 2006 study conducted by the MPSC, found Michigan's deregulation model was so flawed that it was "impossible for regulated utilities to compete on a level playing field" with the alternate electric suppliers.

Instead of returning to full regulation or embracing full deregulation, the MPSC proposed a legislative solution that would authorize the commission to grant a certificate of need for the construction of a new baseload generation facility. Previous law required a utility to prove the need for a new power plant after it was built, making it possible that, if forecast demand fell, a plant could be rejected after the utility had already invested the money to construct it. The MPSC plan also proposed making it more difficult for customers to switch providers, and it required customers that chose unregulated alternative suppliers to bear some of the costs associated with the construction of new generating plants.

THE BALANCED ENERGY INITIATIVE

Three months after the MPSC released its proposal, Consumers Energy responded with a plan of its own, called the Balanced Energy Initiative (BEI). Consumers Energy warned that if new generating plants weren't built in the state, Michigan customers would pay more for electricity in coming decades, and it committed to investing billions of dollars to make sure capacity was available to meet demand.

The BEI invoked a diverse set of strategies: improving energy efficiency, employing demand management, using more renewable energy sources, upgrading existing generation resources and building new power plants. Specifically, Consumers Energy pledged that between 2008 and 2018, almost two-thirds of the projected resource needs would be met by a combination of new renewable energy sources

and peak load reductions achieved by new energy efficiency and demand management programs.

"Our guiding principle was, and still is, that a balanced and diverse approach to resources is essential; there should be no dominant reliance on any one kind of fuel or technology," says Bill Garrity, an architect of the BEI who retired in 2012 as Consumers Energy's senior vice president for energy initiatives and strategy. "The BEI brought all those things together

into one framework, rather than having them separated and not necessarily looked at in a totally integrated fashion."

Within months of introducing the Balanced Energy Initiative, Consumers Energy closed on the purchase of a 930-megawatt, natural gas-fired power plant in Zeeland to help meet peak needs. But new baseload generating plants—the workhorses of electric supply—still had to be built to serve customers.

For that, in September 2007, Consumers

Energy announced that it would build a new clean-coal power plant at Karn-Weadock. As Stephen Wawro, manager of new generation initiatives, wrote later in a letter to the MPSC, it would be a "high efficiency, advanced supercritical pulverized coal design that will use proven, state-of-the-art technology in all aspects of its operations, including the latest and best available technology to control emissions." The 830-megawatt plant would create 1,800 construction jobs, about 2,500 indirect jobs and more than 100 permanent jobs once it became operational in 2017.

Wawro's enthusiasm and the state's growing need for power notwithstanding, the project would never come to pass, in part because of very bad timing: the plant was announced just as the United States was entering the worst economic crisis since the Great Depression, a two-year recession that would be followed by a long, slow slog to recovery. In May 2010, the company announced that it would not develop

Consumers Energy purchased the Zeeland combined-cycle generating facility in 2007. Powered by natural gas, Zeeland has a generating capacity of 930 megawatts, enough to power a community of about 800,000 people.

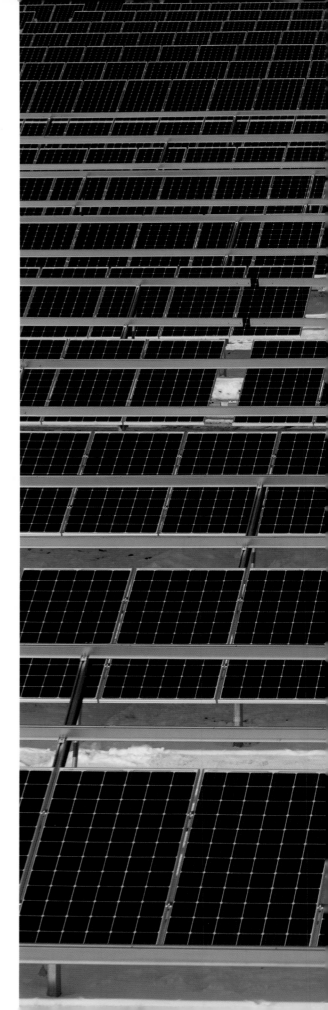

Renewable energy such as wind and solar played an ever greater role when Michigan adopted landmark energy reforms in 2008. Consumers Energy would later develop wind and solar farms, including, below, Cross Winds Energy Park in Michigan's Thumb region and two university-based Solar Gardens power plants, including one at Grand Valley State University, opposite.

the plant. It cited reduced customer demand for electricity because of the financial crisis, anticipated lower natural gas prices driven by developments in shale gas recovery technology, and a projected surplus of generating capacity in the Midwest.

PREPARING FOR THE FUTURE

On Oct. 6, 2008, renewable energy gained a stronger foothold in Michigan when then-Gov. Jennifer Granholm signed the Clean, Renewable and Efficient Energy Act, which required all Michigan electric providers to derive at least 10 percent of the power they supply to retail customers from renewable energy by 2015. The renewable standard was part of a broader, landmark energy law that streamlined Michigan's regulatory process, paved the way for energy efficiency gains, provided stability to enable major utility investments and helped protect customers from market volatility.

Clearly, the future of the energy business would be replete with new technologies and would require innovative thinking and new ways of generating power, getting it to customers and helping them efficiently manage its use. The skills that had driven a 150-year-old industry needed renewal of their own.

On Aug. 28, 2008, Consumers Energy dedicated a $5 million, state-of-the-art training center intended to bring the skills of the company's workforce into the 21st century, with a focus on renewable energy. The Marshall Training Center was built on the site of a former complex near Battle Creek where, for nearly 20 years, Consumers Energy had trained line and

substation workers to safely perform their jobs.

As in days past, line apprentices visit the 41-acre center to complete the nearly 10,000 hours of on-the-job training and classroom work they need to reach the post of journeyman lineworker. They splice cables and fix transformers in a model substation vault 10 feet underground; navigate high-wire electric distribution tasks atop 45-foot-high training poles; and set up faults in the meter socket at a de-energized substation, then look for errors to ensure that they are taking the proper voltage. They combine in-classroom and Internet-enabled distance learning to get up to speed on wind turbines, photovoltaic arrays, hooking up privately owned renewable systems to the grid, and the challenges of storing and distributing renewable energy. About 2,000 Consumers Energy employees pass through the new training center every year.

Strong and focused again, the company was preparing for the energy marketplace of the future, striding ahead with ever more confidence.

In May 2010, it had a bold new CEO to lead the way when Dave Joos retired as president and CEO of CMS Energy and Consumers Energy and was succeeded by John Russell, who had served as president and chief operating officer of Consumers Energy.

Although Consumers Energy had completed a remarkable turnaround from its near-ruin eight years earlier, Russell wasn't satisfied. "Good is not good enough," was his motto, and he immediately announced a set of goals in areas such as safety, cost, customer satisfaction, reliability, sustainability and environmental stewardship.

David Mengebier, senior vice president of governmental, regulatory and public affairs, admits that at the time, the company had no idea how it was going to meet those goals. But, he says, "Setting aspirational goals we don't know how we'll achieve, and then working to achieve them—that's what has made this company great."

Opposite, the Marshall Training Center provides outdoor training facilities, an indoor arena with 45-foot high training poles and renewable energy components that include two small-scale wind turbines and a fixed-panel solar array. Above, John Russell, center, then president and CEO of Consumers Energy, and other company executives rang the closing bell at the New York Stock Exchange in 2012 to celebrate the company's 125th anniversary and the 65th anniversary of the company's stock listing.

Lake Winds Energy Park, Consumers Energy's first wind farm, stands as a symbol of the company's commitment to clean, reliable and affordable energy.

7: Renewable

Consumers Energy's balanced generation portfolio taps renewable sources, including wind and solar, along with electricity produced by baseload generating facilities such as the coal-fired Campbell plant, above, near Lake Michigan.

When the charismatic and personable John Russell took over as Consumers Energy's president and CEO, Frank Johnson was one of the first to take the measure of the new leader's effect on morale. Johnson was senior vice president of energy operations at the time, which meant that he oversaw all of the company's operations except generation. Nearly two-thirds of Consumers Energy's 7,300 employees were under his supervision.

Johnson says employees, while initially war-weary and skeptical, were relieved to know that Consumers Energy was again focused on a business they valued, had a strategy they could believe in and had a CEO who was open, available and eager to listen.

"Russell was very visible from day one," Johnson says. "Employees would call him directly, and if he was in the office, he'd take the call—not like most CEOs you hear about. If I was at a regional headquarters and said something someone didn't like, by the time I got back to my office, I'd hear from Russell: 'You were in Harrison yesterday, right? Did you say this?' I think if employees feel that they can call and vent to the top, it reduces tension. They want to know that the top guy hears them."

John Butler, senior vice president of human resources and shared services, says one of Russell's distinguishing traits is his respect for the union and the employees it represents. "He goes into every labor negotiation with the assumption that the person on the other side of the table is trying to do the right thing for their workforce," Butler says. "The union has come to recognize that they have supportive partners in the company."

When Russell became CEO, Consumers Energy had spent nearly a decade either in the throes of a financial crisis or recovering from crisis. People were tired of constantly putting out fires, and it was time to move on, to look ahead with a long-term horizon.

"We had been getting by year by year," Russell says, "but we had to return to putting as much focus on operational excellence as on the bottom line."

Where Ken Whipple's mantra for Consumers Energy had been "back to basics" and Dave Joos' "building on the basics," Russell's was

Then-Consumers Energy President and CEO John Russell and his team dig into a strategy session based on his efforts to apply breakthrough thinking companywide to its core business.

"breakthrough thinking." Under that banner, he sought an innovative path to make Consumers Energy number-one in its industry—setting high goals and maintaining day-to-day focus on them even if the journey to the top might take 10 years or more.

"Good was not enough," says Russell, whose intensity of focus and attention to detail match that of his friend, Michigan State basketball coach Tom Izzo. "We had to be the very best utility we could be: in safety, in operational excellence, in taking care of our customers and in keeping our rates competitive. That meant doing a lot of things well at the same time."

Russell explains that the utility business is nearly uniform throughout the country, with virtually every utility having access to capital and building similar power plants and distribution systems. "But what separates the best companies," he says, "is their mind-set: how they think about managing the business, working with the customer and making sure the assets they invest in are for the customers' benefit."

Step by step, Russell's seemingly audacious goals moved within reach. Employees rallied behind the aspiration to make Consumers Energy best in class, producing significant improvements in reliability, energy efficiency, customer satisfaction, environmental impact, cost reduction and—especially important—their own satisfaction on the job.

Consumers Energy has delivered consistent financial performance for investors during the past decade.

SMART ENERGY

To simultaneously improve energy efficiency, save customers money and lower costs, Consumers Energy is replacing conventional electric meters with upgraded meters featuring new technology. The plan is to replace every one of the nearly 2 million meters in its territory by the end of 2017.

Every upgraded meter contains a cellular card that securely sends usage information to Consumers Energy; no longer does a meter reader have to traipse through a customer's yard. As many as 720 reads can be taken of every meter every month, improving billing accuracy and eliminating estimated bills. Furthermore, customers can use a web portal to view and analyze the usage information provided by the meter, allowing them to manage their use more wisely and shift consumption to times when power is less costly.

The new meters were deployed as the first part of a longer-term effort to create a smart grid that will give the company greater insight into the grid's performance and more efficient management of the system. A smart grid will make it possible for the company to precisely gauge customers' use, allocate power and regulate voltage based on actual demand with greater speed and efficiency than ever, with more useful information and at lower cost.

As Garrick Rochow, Consumers Energy's senior vice president of distribution and customer operations, explains, "In the past when we put electricity on the grid, we've had to use substations to boost the voltage so that by the time it gets to the last person on the line, they still have sufficient voltage. That meant a lot of inefficiency. Now we see the voltage for every single customer and optimize the entire grid, using advances in voltage indicators, capacitors and regulators on the system to reduce waste." He says that smart grid technology, which should be fully rolled out by 2019, has the potential to significantly increase efficiency and reduce cost.

Taken together, all of the investments in efficiency made by Consumers Energy between 2009 and 2016 have added up to about 450

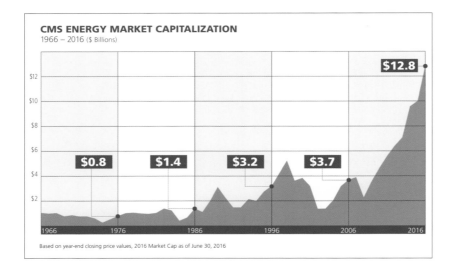

CMS ENERGY MARKET CAPITALIZATION
1966 – 2016 ($ Billions)

$12.8

$0.8 $1.4 $3.2 $3.7

1966   1976   1986   1996   2006   2016

Based on year-end closing price values, 2016 Market Cap as of June 30, 2016

"negawatts"—the equivalent of the output of a good-sized power plant that the company doesn't have to build.

GIVING CUSTOMERS WHAT THEY WANT

Recognizing that winning back the loyalty of customers and meeting their needs was crucial to the company's short- and long-term success, Consumers Energy began asking customers what was most important to them in a utility. The company then put in place a process for analyzing and prioritizing the needs that customers articulated, taking action to meet those needs and measuring progress in doing so.

"We built a customer council of officers from across the company who would own our customer satisfaction performance," says Patti Poppe, who as vice president of customer experience led the initiative beginning in 2011. "We added people to the team who had external customer background and experience, who could translate our customer satisfaction feedback into action plans and work with our legacy employees to teach them what customers really care about. We always had the latent capability to do this. We just didn't know the right things to focus on."

At the top of the list: communication. Customers didn't want to be surprised by an unexpectedly high bill. They didn't want to have to keep calling Consumers Energy to get

Upgraded meter technology helps customers manage their electricity use and predict the size of their bills before they arrive.

an outage resolved. They wanted problems resolved promptly and wanted to know when to expect the power to come back on. In response, Consumers Energy developed a system of online and push notifications designed to keep customers informed and improve communication with the utility. Customers can now receive automatic notices if their energy use is unusually high, along with tips for lowering consumption. They can get similar notices advising of approaching storms or power outages, plus suggestions for actions they can take for their safety or convenience.

"Customers are pretty resilient and understand that when bad weather comes through, there may be power disruptions," Garrick Rochow says. "But the key to satisfaction during these situations is information. We send out push notifications explaining the area of the outage and the estimated time when power will be restored, as well as follow-ups and verifications that service is back on."

By 2015, Consumers Energy was spending more than $150 million a year to improve reliability: inspecting and replacing poles and cross-arms, replacing transformers and insulators, adding new electric wires and

Service in the 21st century electricity business means responsiveness, proactive communication and giving customers tools they can use to become more energy-efficient. The company's mobile-responsive website, above, allows customers to report outages and check the status of restoration efforts via their smartphones. Opposite, the company's Appliance Service Plan covers service calls, labor and parts for a variety of appliance repairs; here, a service technician prepares for a call on her truck-mounted tablet.

Support for Michigan

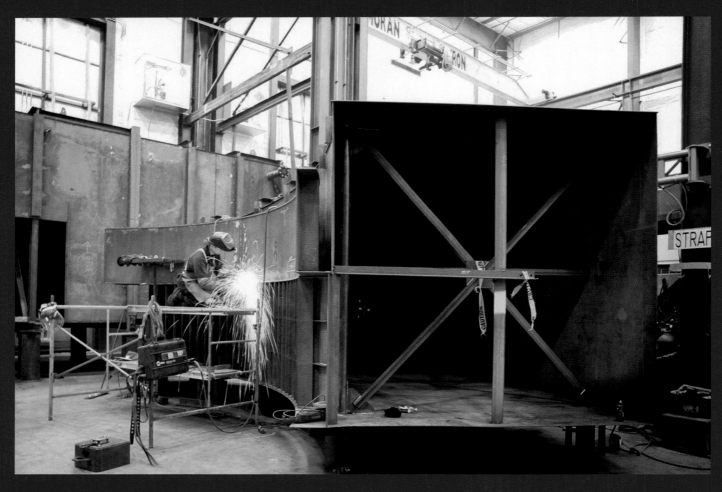

Sue Bursteinowicz had operated Aaron's Fabrication of Steel, Tube and Welding in the Lake St. Clair town of Chesterfield for years, but she was looking to give her company a kick-start. In July 2014, she got the boost she needed when she visited the Consumers Energy Suppliers Summit in Flint. On its own or in partnership with other Michigan-based businesses, Consumers Energy holds the summits every year in an effort to find new in-state suppliers.

"It's kind of like speed dating for businesses," says Dan Malone, senior vice president of energy resources for Consumers Energy. In advance of every summit, Consumers Energy posts its current needs and specifications for products and services on the Michigan Economic Development Corporation's website. Principals of Michigan

businesses can apply through the website for opportunities to make one-on-one pitches to company representatives at a summit.

There were 10 summits between the program's inception in 2011 and June 2016. Attendance ranged from 75 vendors to as many as 2,000. About 10 percent of the companies that attended earned a contract with one of the sponsoring companies.

Bursteinowicz is one of nearly 400 successful applicants to date. She had never done work for Consumers Energy and didn't get an opportunity to bid after participating in the 2013 summit. Undeterred, she went to Flint the following year and got a peek at Consumers Energy's requirements for electric-meter brackets.

"She did the fabricating in her garage, made prototypes and took them to our

A $19 million contract with Moran Iron Works, a leading manufacturer in northern Michigan, is one example of Consumers Energy's commitment to the state's Pure Michigan Business Connect Initiative. The contract to fabricate clean-air equipment for Consumers Energy's power plants allowed Moran to expand its metal fabrication operations and create 75 new jobs.

engineering group, which gave her the opportunity to bid on a long-term agreement," Malone says. "She now has a multimillion-dollar contract with us."

The summit has helped Consumers Energy deliver on an ambitious commitment through the state's Pure Michigan Business Connect initiative to increase the amount of business it does with Michigan-based companies by $1 billion over five years, above the $2 billion it already spends every year as one of the state's largest purchasers of goods and services. Consumers Energy fulfilled that promise in April 2015, a year ahead of schedule, and promptly raised the pledge to an additional $5 billion between 2015 and 2020.

"We call it the circle," says John Russell, who became chairman of the boards of CMS Energy and Consumers Energy in May 2016. "We spend the money, competitively priced products come in, and the quality is beyond belief."

Consumers Energy has also worked closely with state and regional economic development partners to attract large employers to Michigan. Company representatives meet with site-selection teams from companies considering relocation, telling them about the advantages of the state's business climate, workforce and infrastructure, and answering any questions about electric and gas service.

"Over the past several years, we've been able to help bring some large national and even international companies to Michigan," says Garrick Rochow, Consumers Energy's senior vice president of distribution and customer operations. Among them:

Brembo, an Italian manufacturer of high-performance automotive brake systems, which brought 250 jobs to Homer with its North American expansion.

Citic Dicastal, a Chinese manufacturer of aluminum alloy wheels, which spent $140 million to build its first North American production facility, in Greenville.

Chilean particle board manufacturer Arauco, which in 2015 announced that it would bring 250 new jobs to Grayling with the construction of a $325 million facility.

Proudly serving
MICHIGAN *for*
125
YEARS

Former President and CEO John Russell and Pat Dillon, president of the Michigan State Utility Workers Council, help break ground on Consumers Energy's $7.5 million Groveland Customer Service Center, completed in 2013.

Part of the company's commitment to Michigan, the center employs 75 people and serves about 114,000 Oakland County gas customers.

Grayling Generating Station, below, uses primarily bark, sawdust and other wood waste to produce electricity, generating enough power for 26,000 average homes. Opposite, the Solar Gardens power plant at Grand Valley State University began operations in June 2016. The 17-acre, 11,200-solar-panel facility provides electricity to customers across the state.

installing new automatic relay equipment. The power was staying on more reliably, and customers were kept better informed of what was happening. The result: in 2015, the national market research firm Cogent Reports ranked Consumers Energy fifth in the nation for customer satisfaction among electric and gas utilities.

TOWARD BALANCED POWER

Among Consumers Energy's commitments as it set its sights more solidly on the future was one made to the sustainability of the planet—to produce and deliver greater amounts of energy from environmentally friendly and renewable sources. About 10 percent of the power that Consumers Energy supplies to customers comes from renewable sources that include wind, landfill gas, biomass, solar, geothermal and hydroelectric facilities. Consumers Energy was

able to meet Michigan's 10 percent renewables standard roughly a year ahead of the state's schedule.

Tougher environmental regulations and a desire to do the right thing pushed utilities such as Consumers Energy ever harder toward more balanced energy portfolios, and several developments of the first decade of the 2000s hastened their move. One was an overwhelming anti-coal sentiment in the country, rooted in the scarcity of supply and the reality that coal as burned in the existing fleet of power plants is a comparatively dirty fuel and causes an unacceptable amount of air pollution. Others included an unexpected ability to extract great quantities of natural gas from underground shale, and technological achievements that made renewable power such as hydroelectricity, wind and solar more efficient, more affordable and easier to store and distribute.

Coal remains a significant source of power in the United States, but major investments in new coal-fired plants seem to be a thing of the past. Advances in renewables technology and the use of techniques such as hydraulic fracturing and horizontal drilling to extract natural gas from Midwestern shale fields have made burning coal both economically and practically unfeasible.

"No one could have foreseen the natural gas supply development in places like the Marcellus and Utica basins in Pennsylvania," says Kip Daly, former executive director of gas management services for Consumers Energy. More than half of the company's natural gas supply used to come from the Gulf Coast, fluctuating with offshore drilling production and the effects of natural disasters such as hurricanes. By 2016, nearly 60 percent of Consumers Energy's natural gas was coming from Ohio and Pennsylvania.

A network of 15 interconnected underground natural gas storage fields—comprising one of the largest such facilities in the country—enables Consumers Energy to buy most of its natural gas supply during the summer, when prices are lowest, saving customers millions of dollars every year.

Among Consumers Energy's commitments as it set its sights more solidly on the future was one made to the sustainability of the planet–to produce and deliver greater amounts of energy from environmentally friendly and renewable sources.

In 2015, the company started a $165 million upgrade to the St. Clair Compressor Station in Ira Township, above. The project was part of a broader investment to enhance the safety and reliability of Consumers Energy's natural gas infrastructure.

In these old gas and oil production fields, wells can be drilled and gas injected into the porous rock; the process is reversed when it's time to take the gas out. During the brutal "polar vortex" cold snap of 2013, Consumers Energy's residential and business customers saved nearly $300 million thanks to stored natural gas, which provides as much as 80 percent of the company's gas supply on the coldest days of the year.

The exponential growth in the availability of natural gas at low prices led Consumers Energy to briefly consider building a 700-megawatt, combined-cycle natural gas plant in the town of Thetford, in Genesee County. Permits were granted, but in early 2014, the plan was deferred in favor of a less costly option: purchasing an existing natural gas plant on Jackson's east side. The price was $155 million, whereas the Thetford plant would cost an estimated $700 million. Thetford was canceled, while Jackson was an affordable solution that came along at the right time.

"It was too good a deal to pass up," Daly says. "It offered tremendous opportunity and value for our customers."

RECHARGING THE BIG BATTERY

By 2005, the turbines of the Ludington Pumped Storage Facility, a hydroelectric peaking plant and one of Consumers Energy's most environmentally clean generation units, needed either a massive overhaul or total replacement.

"The original turbines were built in the days of slide rules and T-squares, and the tolerances and thresholds weren't as tight as we can make them today with technology that didn't exist almost 50 years ago," explains Bill Schoenlein, the plant's manager. Overhauled or new turbines would keep them running reliably while enabling the facility to generate far more power far more efficiently.

Given the high cost of restoration, the company decided on replacement. In February 2011, Consumers Energy announced that all six of Ludington's turbines would be replaced with new, higher-powered models, allowing the plant to increase its generating capacity

from 1,872 megawatts to approximately 2,172 megawatts. The plan, and its execution, would be an engineering marvel nearly equal to that of Ludington's original construction.

Japanese manufacturer Toshiba, one of only a handful of companies in the world that could handle such a task, was chosen to build the new turbines. Each one—at 270 tons and 27.5 feet in diameter, physically the largest motors in the world—took three years to build. The original turbines had six blades; the replacements would have nine. More blades meant more energy, which accounts for part of their increased capacity. The blades would also be about 16 inches longer than the previous ones; their ability to push more water would reduce the time needed to fill the upper reservoir from 11.5 hours to 9.5 hours.

One by one, the new turbines made the month-long journey across the ocean by barge from Toshiba's subsidiary in Hangzhou, China. After all the pieces of the giant stators—non-rotating components of a turbine—arrived in western Michigan, the turbines and two 410-ton

Coal, above, being unloaded at the now-retired Cobb facility in April 2016, remains an important part of Consumers Energy's balanced energy portfolio.

overhead gantry cranes were assembled on site at Ludington's North Fabrication Building, which had been built especially for the purpose.

Unit 2, the first turbine to set out from China, arrived on Sept. 9, 2013, and one new unit is being put into service every year. Installation of the entire set of new turbines is expected to be complete in 2018.

The new turbines are designed to provide affordable, sustainable energy for at least 30 years before needing another overhaul.

WIND, SUN AND WASTE

Standing watch over the installation of the new turbines were 56 giants—the 476-foot-tall wind turbines of Lake Winds Energy Park, Consumers Energy's first major investment in company-owned wind power. Located on miles of farmland in Summit and Riverton townships, Lake Winds is close enough to Ludington for a brisk hike between the two sites.

"We opted to go with the Ludington area first, principally because the pumped storage facility is there and the major transmission infrastructure is there, which means we have the capacity to easily take the generation from a wind farm onto the grid," says Dennis Marvin, Consumers Energy's community engagement manager for the area. Getting a steady supply of renewable power, which is often generated in remote areas, onto the grid is a challenge for utilities, and Consumers Energy was fortunate to have a pre-existing solution.

Lake Winds Energy Park began operating at the end of 2012. Each of its 56 turbines is sunk 12 feet into the Michigan earth, anchored with 600 tons of concrete and two tons of rebar—all invisible from above. Atop every turbine sits an anemometer that transmits wind speed and direction to a controller, which turns the blades to face the wind.

Each turbine can produce up to 1.8 megawatts of electricity annually, giving the park a capacity of about 100 megawatts. Variable wind conditions mean that the facility can usually generate about a third of that

Workers, opposite, attach the first of three blades to the hub of a rotor on a turbine at Lake Winds Energy Park. When aligned, the blade bolts will go through holes in the hub (or pitch bearing), and washers and nuts will be attached to hold the blade in place.

capacity on any given day. In theory, Lake Winds could provide all of the electric power needed for the residents and businesses of Mason and Manistee counties.

Consumers Energy began operating its second wind farm, the 111-megawatt Cross Winds Energy Park, located in Tuscola County in the heart of Michigan's Thumb, at the end of 2014.

The sun is yet another source of power for Consumers Energy customers. Under a program begun in 2014 called Solar Gardens, the company is building solar farms in western Michigan. Consumers Energy completed its first two installations—a 17-acre site with 11,000 solar panels at Grand Valley State University in Allendale and an 8.5-acre site with 3,900 panels at Western Michigan University in Kalamazoo—by the spring of 2016; both were operational that fall. Customers who subscribe to the Solar Gardens program get credits on their bills for the energy produced.

GOODBYE TO THE CLASSIC SEVEN

As the era of wind and solar power began, another was coming to an end. After more than 60 years in operation, Consumers Energy's seven oldest coal plants—two thirds of its coal fleet, capable of generating nearly 1,000 megawatts of electricity—were shut down in April 2016.

The move made economic and

environmental sense. The retirement of the Classic Seven, as they were affectionately known, would help Michigan cut carbon emissions and improve air quality, and it had become expensive to run the plants in compliance with stricter environmental rules and with less expensive sources of fuel, such as natural gas, available. Consumers Energy was already spending more than $1.1 billion on environmental upgrades to three units at its newer coal-fired facilities: the Campbell plant and two units at Karn in Bay City.

Only one other utility in the U.S. at the time was retiring a higher percentage of its coal generation, but that didn't make the shutdowns any less painful. The oldest of the Classic Seven then in operation, J.R. Whiting Units 1, 2 and 3, near Luna Pier, generated their first electricity during the Truman administration. Along with B.C. Cobb 4 and 5 in Muskegon and J.C. Weadock 7 and 8 in Hampton Township, Whiting had provided reliable, affordable energy for decades. Shortly before the shutdown, Whiting's Unit 3 set a company record by operating continuously for 679 days, the sixth-longest run for a U.S. power plant.

"They have been operating quite well for such a long time, and that makes it difficult to say that we have to shut them down when they could continue to operate well into the future," says Tim Sparks, vice president of energy supply operations. "But we had to look at the long term. It just didn't make sense to spend a tremendous amount of money—probably hundreds of millions of dollars each—to keep them operational and compliant with environmental regulations for maybe a decade more at most."

The plants had also been pillars of their communities, providing jobs, tax revenue and economic horsepower for generations. Consumers Energy worked to minimize the impact of their closure on those communities, and it took that responsibility seriously. Several years in advance, the company began working with local leaders to help them prepare for new sources of revenue and employment.

"In Muskegon, for example, there is a deep water port that comes into the Cobb plant,

Consumers Energy retired its aging, Classic Seven coal-fired plants in 2016, bringing an end to more than 75 years of history at those facilities.

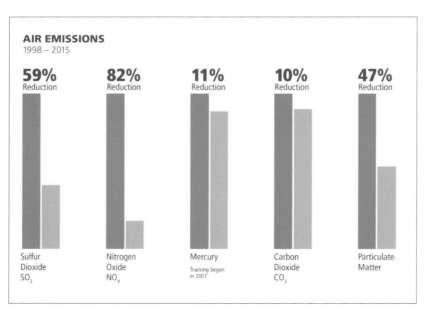

AIR EMISSIONS
1998 – 2015

59% Reduction — Sulfur Dioxide SO$_2$

82% Reduction — Nitrogen Oxide NO$_x$

11% Reduction — Mercury (Tracking began in 2007)

10% Reduction — Carbon Dioxide CO$_2$

47% Reduction — Particulate Matter

where we've been bringing in about a million tons of coal a year," Sparks says. "The Army Corps of Engineers won't continue to dredge the port if there isn't a replacement level of commerce to make up for the closure of Cobb."

Consumers Energy sponsored economic impact studies, which found that investing to expand the Port of Muskegon for a container-ship terminal was one way to generate jobs and pump up the economy.

To generate commercial development in the areas around Cobb, Whiting and Weadock, the studies suggested options for agribusiness centers, shipping and storage facilities, or an eco-industrial manufacturing center in which businesses cooperate with each other and share

resources to reduce waste and pollution and to achieve sustainable development.

While some sad sentimentality and the very real challenge of revitalizing communities accompanied the farewell to the Classic Seven, their closure has done what was needed for the present and future health of the planet: the shutdown reduced Consumers Energy's carbon footprint by 25 percent, air emissions by 40 percent and water use by 40 percent.

"The air in Michigan today is cleaner than it's ever been in my lifetime," says John Russell. "Our commitment to leave it better than we found it helped make that possible. Every Consumers Energy employee can be proud of that."

Employees who worked at the Classic Seven generating plants cherished their friendships with co-workers and a family atmosphere that was fostered over many decades.

Giving Back

Support for the communities that Consumers Energy serves is a tradition nearly as old as the company itself. After founder W.A. Foote's death in 1915, his wife, Ida, donated the land on East Avenue in Jackson on which Foote Hospital—now Henry Ford Allegiance Health—was built.

For most of Consumers Energy's history, charitable support was dependent largely on the company's own financial health, and its commitment wavered greatly from year to year. That was especially the case between 1970 and 1990, when earnings spiked and dipped wildly. To provide consistency in support for its communities, the company created the Consumers Power Foundation (now the Consumers Energy Foundation) in 1990.

Carolyn Bloodworth, the foundation's secretary treasurer, says of those roller-coaster decades, "There were times when we had made charitable commitments we could not honor, and we never wanted to repeat that."

The foundation's priorities are education, particularly in science, technology, engineering and math (STEM); environment; community, civic and cultural development; and social welfare. In 2015, Consumers Energy, the foundation and employees contributed $6.6 million to Michigan nonprofits. Recent grants from the foundation have supported organizations as diverse as Kids Food Basket, providing nutritious meals for children in Grand Rapids, Muskegon and Holland; the Community Foundation of Greater Flint, to support early childhood education in Flint; FIRST in Michigan, supporting robotics programs across the state; and the Saginaw Bay Watershed Initiative Network, working to improve the quality of life in the watershed, focusing on land and water resources,

Consumers Energy employees give back to their communities in countless ways, including building or renovating houses for Habitat for Humanity.

In 2015, Walk for Warmth events raised almost $200,000 for heating assistance to help people in need stay warm through the cold Michigan winters. Consumers Energy matches all Walk for Warmth funds raised by employees and participating family and friends.

education, sustainable agriculture, and habitat restoration and protection.

Working with The Salvation Army, Consumers Energy created the PeopleCare program in 1983 to help families, seniors and neighbors in times of crisis. Donations to PeopleCare made by Consumers Energy customers and employees serve needs that people may have in an emergency, such as for groceries, shoes for a growing child, prescriptions, and rent or a house payment.

During the difficult years of 2002 and 2003, Consumers Energy was in no position to be making charitable contributions. But Ken Whipple and his team devised an innovative way to continue funding for the United Way. CMS Energy donated a 1.5 percent interest in the ownership of its portfolio of international assets to the United Way of Jackson County—"all these assets we were soon to sell," says Bloodworth. "Every time a sale would happen,

the United Way would receive the proceeds" according to its share in the portfolio. Over time, the United Way reaped more than $10 million from this arrangement.

For the past two decades, employees and retirees who volunteer at least 45 hours a year in their communities have been able to apply for grants from Consumers Energy for the charity they support through the company's Volunteer Investment Program (VIP).

"We have Little League coaches, scout leaders, nonprofit board members, booster club and parent teacher association members, 4-H leaders, mentors for robotics teams—about 600 people apply for grants annually," Bloodworth says. "These are smaller grants, but $300 buys a lot of badges and camper scholarships for a Boy Scout troop."

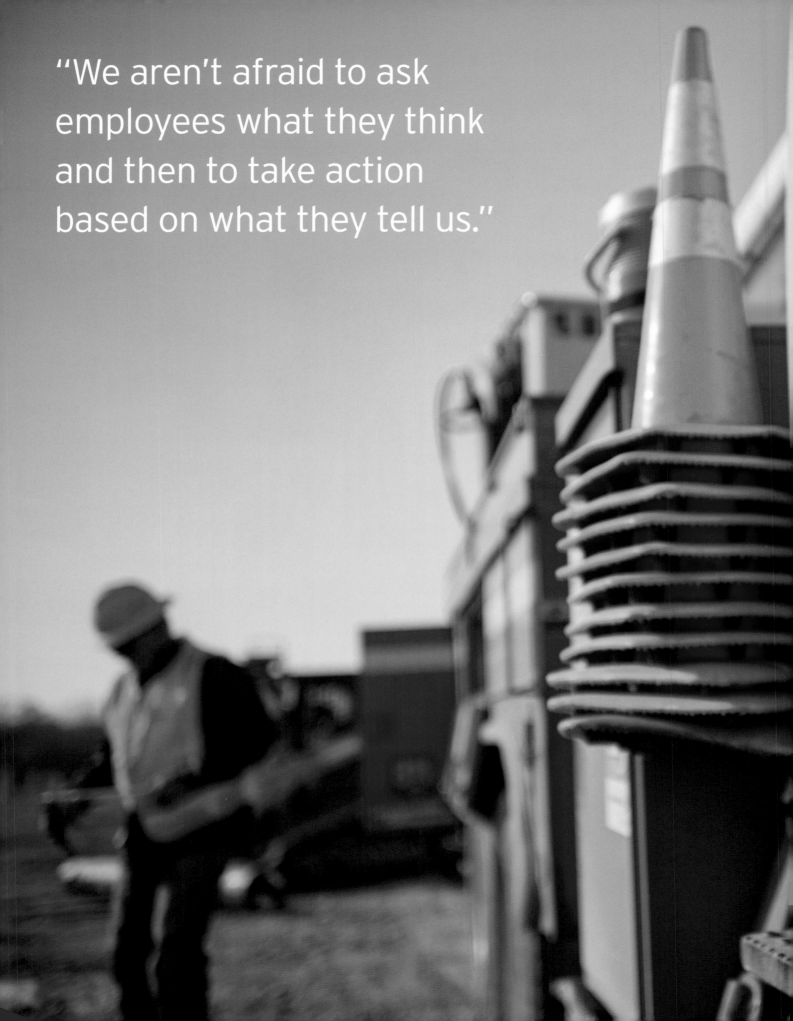

"We aren't afraid to ask employees what they think and then to take action based on what they tell us."

STEADILY COMING AROUND

It would be an overstatement to say employees immediately embraced the ambitious goals set out by John Russell and that they just picked themselves up and rallied optimistically for a renaissance. In fact, says Merri Jo Bales, former executive director of strategy development, communication and integration, "People almost openly scoffed."

It's true that Consumers Energy was no longer on the verge of bankruptcy, but it was hardly in good shape.

"People were thinking, 'Are you kidding me?'" Bales says. "We were in the fourth quartile in customer satisfaction and the worst in reliability among our peers. We were nowhere near where we needed to be." Employees knew better than anyone how much improvement was needed for a recovery, and they needed proof that their new leader was serious about change and that his ideas would pay off. They needed to believe.

Bales says one of the keys to the recovery's success was that "John did not back down in the slightest. By setting goals that were so bold, it forced people to have to think beyond, 'Let's do just what we did yesterday but a little bit better.'"

Consumers Energy conducted its first employee engagement survey in 2004, seeking to know how involved and enthusiastic employees were about the company and about their work. Some might have said that was the worst possible time to start asking people at Consumers Energy what they thought about their employer. But the company genuinely wanted to know what employees thought and what it could do to improve things; it also sought a baseline against which to measure future improvement.

"We were just coming out of our lowest point as a company," says Fern Griesbach, former executive director of human resources. "A lot of businesses would say, 'That's not the time to ask employees how engaged they are.' But we took a different approach, believing that we needed to ask our employees how we could make the company better."

The results of the early surveys were predictably gloomy.

In 2016, President and CEO Patti Poppe, holding hardhat, was named one of the 100 Most Influential Women in Michigan by *Crain's Detroit Business*. Here, she's joined by a growing team of the company's female leaders, who work daily to encourage innovation and earn customers' business. Poppe's strategy to build on the company's success is called the "CE Way"—a commitment to safety, quality, cost and delivery.

"We asked people what kind of service provider they thought we were for customers and whether they would recommend us," Griesbach says. "When we first started the surveys, people didn't think we served customers very well."

It wasn't overnight, but the turnaround in attitude was eventually dramatic. By 2015, Consumers Energy's employee engagement ranked at 78 percent–significantly higher than any other utility and higher even than companies listed on many national best-places-to-work lists. More telling was the survey's participation rate: most companies struggle to get even half of their workforces to take time to answer such surveys, but Consumers Energy's engagement surveys get a 70 percent response rate.

"We aren't afraid to ask employees what they think and then to take action based on what they tell us," Griesbach says. "That's made a difference in making this a place where

people are excited to come to work."

Russell instituted regular video broadcasts and posted blog entries for employees to read on the company's intranet. He addressed a wide range of topics, from open discussion of company decisions and changes to developments in rate cases to the latest in new plant construction.

"We've come a long way in being transparent as a company, so employees know what our priorities are and how their contributions fit in," Griesbach says.

PROUD TO WEAR THE COLORS

As evidence of the company's faith in its employees and the unions that represent many of them, when Consumers Energy opened a new training center in June 2014, it put the responsibility for running it in the hands of the Utility Workers Union of America (UWUA) Power for America Training Trust Fund. The 10,000-square-foot center in Potterville, southwest of Lansing, features seven classrooms and laboratories where as many as 2,500 employees can gain and sharpen skills in meter reading, gas appliance repair and other natural gas- and electricity-related service fields.

"Establishing the union as the body that does training for the company is game-changing," says John Butler of human resources and shared services. "This positions them as a real supplier of talent and builds a stronger path for the future. In recent years, we've watched the decline of unions, and this has the potential to reverse that and reposition the union as a value-creating part of the talent chain."

Pat Dillon, a journeyman lineworker at Consumers Energy and president of the Michigan State Utility Workers Council, said the union has established a high bar for the quality of training at the new center. In a press release in which the company announced the center's opening, Dillon said, "We want to set the standard of excellence for training utility workers to do their work to the best of their abilities."

Another key to employees' enthusiasm: a relentless focus on safety, made most visible in a Stop the Job campaign that cut reportable safety incidents in half between 2009 and 2014. At first, veteran employees were just as dismissive of the safety effort as they were of Russell's other goals. They'd seen similar claims go nowhere in the past.

"It took some convincing, but the process actually changed the way we're thinking," says Frank Rand, environmental and chemistry lead at the J.R. Whiting coal plant.

Today, one of the busiest spots in Consumers Energy's flagship building in downtown Jackson is the company store, where employees can buy everything from polo shirts to jackets, ball caps and gym bags sporting the familiar blue-and-green energy-shield logo. "Today, just about everybody's proud to wear those colors," Merri Jo Bales says.

To hold itself to the promises it made for safety, reliability, customer satisfaction and environmental stewardship, Consumers Energy began publishing an annual accountability report in 2013. While showing that the results of Consumers Energy's efforts are generally positive—for example, in 2015, emissions and safety incidents were down dramatically while productivity and energy efficiency hit all-time highs—the reports identify areas for improvement. For example, employee safety incidents, while still at record lows, ticked up slightly from 2013 to 2014.

By 2015, Consumers Energy had become the second-most-trusted combination utility in the Midwest and the third-most-trusted in the nation, according to industry analysis by Cogent Reports. The company was also ranked highest in the Midwest for environmental performance—a hard-won distinction earned as the company balanced its energy portfolio. Consumers Energy projected that in 2016, 24 percent of its energy would come from coal and

The heart of Consumers Energy has always been its people, from the intrepid charters of the Au Sable River in the 1880s to the lineworkers, customer service specialists and engineers of today. Proud to wear the Consumers Energy colors, they bring skill, passion and dedication to their work—helping to deliver the promise of a clean, sustainable energy future for Michigan.

34 percent from natural gas, with the remainder generated by renewable sources, pumped storage, nuclear and oil.

A NEW ERA OF LEADERSHIP

In July 2016, after leading employees to turn seemingly unachievable goals into daily reality at Michigan's largest utility, John Russell retired as president and CEO to focus solely on his work as chairman of the boards of Consumers Energy and CMS Energy, a role he assumed in May 2016. Consumers Energy's market capitalization had

increased from $3.4 billion to as high as a record $12.74 billion in Russell's tenure. Customers were measurably more satisfied and employees more engaged than ever.

Russell handed the keys to a Jackson native and true daughter of Consumers Energy: Patti Poppe, whose father worked for Consumers Energy for three decades. Colleagues describe Poppe, former vice president of customer service and senior vice president of distribution operations, engineering and transmission, as a visionary, a problem-solver and a strategic

Over the past 130 years, Consumers Energy has built the electricity and natural-gas infrastructure that powers many of Michigan's cities, communities and farms. The company has survived hardship, learned difficult lessons and returned from the brink stronger every time. The Consumers Energy of today is a company with unlimited vision, potential and a determination to live up to its promise and commitment to its customers and employees—now and for generations to come.

thinker—in other words, a lot like W.A. and J.B. Foote, who founded the predecessor of Consumers Energy 130 years ago.

Poppe doesn't take the company's renewal and recent success for granted, and she knows Consumers Energy will have to work hard, day after day, to earn the faith and trust of its employees and the business of its customers.

"Up in my office, I keep a newspaper clipping from 2011, with a headline about Consumers Energy ranking last in the Midwest for satisfaction among business customers," Poppe says. "We can't become complacent."

In preparing for her new role, Poppe went on what she called a "Let's DOET Tour" (DOET stands for distribution operations, engineering and transmission), beginning in the spring of 2015. Visiting 45 Consumers Energy locations throughout Michigan, she met many of the company's 4,000 front-line employees. Her takeaway: "I see how hard our people work to deliver what we promise to our customers," Poppe says. "That's where our next generation of success will come from."

Acknowledgments

Creating this Book

The author's research was based primarily on personal interviews, company archive materials and media accounts. *Future Builders, The Story of Michigan's Consumers Power Company*, McGraw-Hill, Inc., 1973, was the main source for all historical material prior to the early 1970s.

Author's Acknowledgments

It's a bit embarrassing to admit that before working on this book, I had never spent any more time in Michigan than brief stopovers in the Detroit airport. Researching the history of Consumers Energy remedied that glaring omission in my travel history, offering the opportunity to explore the beauty of the upper Lake Michigan shoreline and experience the warmth and friendliness of downtown Jackson. Clear to me, everywhere I went, was just how much Consumers Energy has contributed to the fabric that binds the state together. It's been a privilege to tell that story.

Introducing me to all things Consumers Energy and all things Michigan were the indefatigable Todd Schulz, Dan Bishop, Dan Gretzner, Andrew Radvansky and Brian Preuss. Todd took me on a remarkable road trip around the Ludington Pumped Storage Facility and Lake Winds Energy Park, and connected me with the extraordinary people whose voices are heard in this book. Andrew and Dan Bishop provided strong leadership, direction and perspective on the company's long and storied history. Dan Gretzner dug through Consumers Energy's rich archives to help me find nuggets of gold that illuminated the people who make up this company. Brian added important insights from his more than 20 years with the company and was invaluable in gathering and selecting imagery.

Many thanks are also due to the dozens of people from the Consumers Energy family who gave their time and shared their stories to make this book rich and real. In particular, I would like to express my gratitude to Patti Poppe, John Russell, Dave Joos, Ken Whipple, David Mengebier, Frank Johnson, Paul Elbert, Tom Elward and Ted Vogel.

—Gina Shaw
October 2016

Consumers Energy Acknowledgments

Editorial team: *Todd Schulz, Dan Bishop, Dan Gretzner, Brian Preuss and Andrew Radvansky.*
Legal team: *Cathy Reynolds, Eric Luoma, Ashley Bancroft, Rick Chambers, Gary Kelterborn,*
    Kelly Hall and Scott Sinkwitts.
Distribution support: *Ron Mason, Dan Brooker and Dan Hoppin.*

About the Author

Gina Shaw yearned to be a writer from the age of 7, when she realized that writing could be an actual job. For the past 20 years, she has specialized in writing about health, medicine and science for trade publications, specialty societies, magazines, universities, medical centers and corporations. With this book, her fifth, she brings her passion for telling a great story to the history of Consumers Energy.

Company Leaders: Presidents/Chief Executive Officers

William A. Foote	1910 – 1915	*President*
Bernard C. Cobb	1915 – 1932	*President*
Timothy A. Kenney	1932 – 1938	*President*
Justin R. Whiting	1941 – 1951	*President*
Daniel E. Karn	1951 – 1960	*President*
James H. Campbell	1960 – 1972	*President*
Alphonse H. Aymond	1972 – 1975	*President*
John B. Selby	1975 – 1985	*President*
William T. McCormick Jr.	1985 – 1987	*President*
Joseph F. Paquette Jr.	1987 – 1988	*President*
Frederick W. Buckman	1988 – 1992	*President*
William T. McCormick Jr.	1989 – 1992	*CEO*
Frederick W. Buckman	1992 – 1994	*President and CEO*
Michael G. Morris	1994 – 1997	*President and CEO*
Victor J. Fryling	1997 – 2000	*President*
William T. McCormick Jr.	2000 – 2002	*President*
David W. Joos	2001 – 2004	*President*
Kenneth A. Whipple	2002 – 2004	*CEO*
David W. Joos	2004 – 2010	*CEO*
John G. Russell	2004 – 2010	*President*
John G. Russell	2010 – 2016	*President and CEO*
Patricia K. Poppe	2016 – present	*President and CEO*

Timeline

1884
A generator placed in William Augustine Foote's flour mill lights 12 streetlights in Adrian. Foote sells the mill and starts an electric company, hiring his brother J.B. as bookkeeper and then chief engineer.

1886
The Footes and Samuel Jarvis form a partnership and secure a franchise agreement to illuminate Jackson with arc lighting. The lights go on in December.

1899
The Trowbridge hydroelectric dam on the Kalamazoo River opens.

1904
Under the name Commonwealth Power Co., W.A. Foote consolidates power companies he has purchased around the state.

1906
Rogers Hydro on the Muskegon River begins generating hydroelectricity.

1907
The Croton Hydro on the Muskegon River begins operating. A 110,000-volt transmission line to Grand Rapids goes live the following year.

Webber Hydro, the company's only hydroelectric plant on the Grand River, is completed.

1911
Cooke Hydro, the first of six hydroelectric plants on the Au Sable River, begins generating electricity. Its 125-mile long, 140,000-volt transmission line to Flint sets a world record.

1912
Five Channels Hydro on the Au Sable River is completed.

1913
The Loud Hydro on the Au Sable River is completed.

1916
The Mio Hydro is completed on the Au Sable River.

1918
Foote Hydro on the Au Sable River begins generating hydroelectricity.

Tippy Hydro is completed on the Manistee River.

1920
Consumers Power begins selling shares of preferred stock to customers for $95 a share, with dividends of $7 a share.

1922
Consumers Power and Michigan Light Company, the former Hodenpyl-Walbridge operations, merge their gas and electric operations into a single entity under the Consumers Power name.

1924
Alcona Hydro on the Au Sable River begins operation.

The company's first coal-fired generation facility, the Saginaw River plant, opens.

1925
The 17,000-kilowatt Hodenpyl Hydro is completed on the Manistee River.

1927
The Mason-Dansville line enters operation, making farmers along that line the nation's first rural power users.

A new headquarters building opens on West Michigan Avenue in Jackson.

1929
Consumers Power becomes part of a network of subsidiaries of a massive holding company called The Commonwealth & Southern Corporation.

1931
The company lays a 40-mile pipeline from natural gas wells in Isabella County to Midland.

Consumers Energy completes its last hydroelectric project, the Hardy Hydro on the Muskegon River.

1940

The J.C. Weadock coal-fired plant on the Saginaw Bay shoreline is dedicated.

1941

The company taps into the Michigan extension of the Panhandle Eastern natural gas pipeline to serve Flint, Owosso, Marshall, Pontiac, Jackson and the Detroit suburbs.

1949

The B.C. Cobb coal-fired plant on the shores of Muskegon Lake opens.

Consumers Power becomes an independent company, separating from Commonwealth & Southern.

1952

The J.R. Whiting coal-fired plant on the shores of Lake Erie begins operation.

1959

The D.E. Karn coal-fired plant in Hampton Township begins generating electricity.

1960

The company completes the Trunkline-Consumers Power pipeline to carry natural gas from the Gulf Coast.

1962

The J.H. Campbell coal-fired plant near Grand Haven begins generating electricity.

Big Rock Point in Charlevoix, the first nuclear plant in Michigan, is built.

1963

Consumers Power acquires the Michigan production properties and exploration leases of Panhandle Eastern.

1967

Plans for the Midland Nuclear Plant are announced.

The company creates the Northern Michigan Exploration Company (NOMECO) subsidiary to pursue gas exploration and production.

1968

Consumers Power, incorporated in Maine in 1910, becomes a Michigan corporation.

1969

The company acquires the Calkins Bridge Dam, also known as Allegan Hydro, on the Kalamazoo River.

1971

The Palisades Nuclear Plant near South Haven comes online.

1973

The Marysville gas reforming plant produces its first supply of synthetic gas. It will shut down six years later.

1973

The Ludington Pumped Storage Facility on Lake Michigan becomes the largest facility of its kind in the world, capable of serving 1.4 million people.

1975

D.E. Karn Unit 3, fueled by natural gas and oil, begins generation.

1984

The company cancels further construction of the Midland Nuclear Plant.

1986

Consumers Power and Dow Chemical Co. announce an agreement to convert the Midland plant to a natural gas cogeneration facility. The plant will go online in 1990.

1987

CMS Energy is formed as a holding company with two principal subsidiaries: Consumers Power and CMS Enterprises, responsible for non-utility and international ventures.

1993

CMS Energy goes global when it, along with partners, acquires Central Termica San Nicolas, a fossil-fuel plant in Argentina. By 1997, the company will own $10 billion worth of energy assets in 17 countries.

1997

Consumers Power changes its name to Consumers Energy Company.

The Big Rock Point Nuclear Plant begins decommissioning after 35 years of safe operation.

2000

The company turns operation of the Palisades Nuclear Plant over to an independent nuclear plant operator.

2001

The company announces an agreement to sell its transmission network to a partnership led by Trans-Elect.

2002

CMS Energy acknowledges that a subsidiary conducted prearranged "round trip" electricity trades. CEO Bill McCormick announces his retirement at the 2002 annual meeting.

CMS Energy sells the Panhandle-Trunkline natural gas system to Southern Union Panhandle Corp. as part of a back-to-basics strategy.

2003

The company sells 15 international assets, garnering $850 million in proceeds.

CMS Energy moves into new headquarters at One Energy Plaza in Jackson.

2004

CMS Energy achieves net positive earnings for the first time in several years, with a net income of $110 million, or 64 cents per share.

Consumers Energy begins major investments in customer service and system maintenance. By 2015, it is spending more than $150 million year to improve reliability.

Consumers Energy conducts its first employee engagement survey.

2005

A major safety summit ushers in a renewed management-union commitment to safety. Reportable safety incidents will drop by more than 78 percent in five years.

2006

With decommissioning completed the previous year, the Big Rock Point nuclear site is restored to its natural state as a 475-acre greenfield on the shore of Lake Michigan.

2007

CMS Energy exits the nuclear generation business when it sells the Palisades Nuclear Plant to Entergy Nuclear Palisades, LLC.

Consumers Energy purchases the Zeeland natural gas combined-cycle generating plant.

2008

Consumers Energy dedicates the Marshall Training Center, focused on upgrading the workforce's skills in renewable energy.

Michigan requires all electric providers in the state to derive at least 10 percent of the power they supply to retail customers from renewable energy by 2015. The company will meet the standard a year ahead of the state's schedule.

2011

Consumers Energy celebrates 125 years of serving Michigan with safe, reliable energy.

2012

Record heat and Michigan's strengthening economy drive customer electric demand on July 17 to an all-time high of 9,086 megawatts.

Lake Winds Energy Park in Mason County begins operation.

The company begins installing upgraded electric meters. The technology upgrade for 1.8 million electric customers, as well as the installation of 200,000 gas communication modules, is expected to be complete by the end of 2017. Full smart-grid technology is expected to be rolled out by 2019.

2014

The company purchases a natural gas-fired power plant in Jackson.

Cross Winds Energy Park in Tuscola County begins operation.

The company begins its Solar Gardens program. Solar power plants at Grand Valley State University in Allendale and Western Michigan University in Kalamazoo began operating in late 2016.

Consumers Energy opens a new training center in Potterville.

2016

Consumers Energy retires seven of its oldest coal-fired power plants.

Index

Bold listings indicate illustrations.

A

Aaron's Fabrication of Steel, Tube and Welding, 132
acquisitions/mergers, 24-26, 29-31, 36, 78, **78-79**, 80, 87, **87**
Adrian, Michigan, 22, **22**, 23, 27
advertising/promotions, 37, **37**, 47, **47**, 54, **54**
Aero-Car Sales Corporation, 36
Africa, 89, 96
Agricultural Electric Council, 91
Al Taweelah A2 plant, 96
Albion, Michigan, 25
Alcona hydroelectric plant, 29
Allen, Robert, 37
Allendale, Michigan, 140
American Electric Power, 82
American Gas Association, 61
American Natural Resources (ANR), 61, 72
American Society of Civil Engineers (ASCE), 49
Anderson, Arthur, 99
Antrim natural gas wells, 87
Appliance Service Plan (ASP), 39, **130-131**
appliances, 32, 36, 37, **37**, 39, 90, **90**
Arabian gulf, 96
Arauco, 133
arc-lighting, 22-26, **22**, **23**
Argentina, 78, 80, 84, **84**, 87, 97-98
Army Corps of Engineers, 141
Atacama Pipeline, 84, **84**, 97
Atomic Energy Act (1954), 36
Atomic Energy Commission (AEC), 54, 55, 57
Au Sable River, 26, **26**, 29, 50, 51, 75, 147
austerity program, 103-104, 108
Australia, 78, 87, 89, 97, 99
Aymond, Al, 106, **107**

B

back to basics strategy, 102-104, **103**, 105, 127
Baker, Don, 50, 51, 92
Balanced Energy Initiative (BEI), 116, 118, 137
Bales, Merri Jo, 145, 147
bankruptcy, 16, 56, 61, 99, 105, 145
Barrett, Andy, 14, **14**, 15
Barrett, Brooke, 15
Barrett, Debbie, **14**
Barrett, Francis W. "Frank," 14, **14**
Barrett, Laurie. *See* Harris, Laurie (Barrett)
Barrett, Mike, **14**
Barrett, Pete, **14**
baseball, 51, 68
Battle Creek, Michigan, 25
Bay City, Michigan, 32, 73, 74, 112, 140

Bay Harbor, 110-111, **110-111**
B.C. Cobb fossil-fuel complex, 36, 45, **45**, 112, 137, **137**, 140-141
Bechtel, 55-56, 57
Big Rock Historical Society, 113
Big Rock Point nuclear plant, 37, 40, **40-41**, 41, 57, 92-94, **92-94**, 112, 113, **113**
Big Rock Point Restoration Project, 93
biomass power, 57, 134, **134**
Bishop, Dan, 61
Black and Veatch, 58
blackout, 10-11, **10**, 13, 16, 108, 112
Blanchard, James, 68
Bloodworth, Carolyn, 60, 142, 143
board of directors, 60, 61, 72, 75, 98, 102, 103, 106, 108, 112
Brazil, 84
breakthrough thinking strategy, 128
Brembo, 133
Brethren, Michigan, 90
Broomfield Township, 32
Brown, James A., 30
build on the basics strategy, 112, 127
Burd, Edward, 51
Bursa-Yalova electric distribution systems, 97
Bursteinowicz, Sue, 132-133
Butler, John, 127, 147

C

California, 95, 99
call center, 108
Campbell, James H. "Jim," 37, 41
Canada, 52
Carmoney, Lisa, 22
Carter, Jimmy, 82
CE Way strategy, 146
Centennial Farm Association, 91
Centennial Farms, 91, **91**
Centrales Termicas San Nicolas, S.A., 84
charitable support, 142-143, **142-143**
Charlevoix, Michigan, 37, 92
Charlotte Gas Company, 30
Chile, 78
China, 137, 138
Citic Dicastal, 133
Citizens Electric Company, 30
Clark, John, 72, 80, 82
Classic Seven coal-fired plants, 140, 141
Clean Air Act (1990), 89
Clean Corporate Citizen designation, 89
Clean, Renewable and Efficient Energy Act, 120
CMS Capital, 110

CMS Energy Corporation, 38, 75, 83, **83**, 84, 86, 87, 89, 94, 96-99, 102-106, 108, 110-112, 123, 133, 148. *See also* acquisitions/mergers

CMS Enterprises Company, 83, 89

CMS Generation Co., 83

CMS Land Company, 110-111

CMS Marketing, Services and Trading Company, 83, 98

CMS Oil and Gas, 84

CMS Panhandle companies, 106

coal/coal power, 13, 16, 30, 32, 36, 39, 45, 47, 57, 64, 69, 78, 96, 97, 112, 113, 119, 126, 134, 137, 140-141, 147. *See also specific plant names*

Cobb, Bernard Capen, 30, 31, 32

cogeneration, 42, 56-57, 60, 62, 64, 77, **77**, 84. *See also* Midland Cogeneration Venture (MCV)

Cogent Reports, 17, 134, 147

Coldwater, Michigan, 39

Colombia, 87

Commonwealth & Southern Corporation, 15, 32, 34

Commonwealth Power Corporation, 26, 27, **27**, 29, **29**, 31

Commonwealth Power Railway & Light Company, 29, 30, 31

communication, 129, 131

Community Foundation of Greater Flint, 142

Congo, 87

Consumers Energy Company (formerly Consumers Power Company)
    beginnings of, 13-17, **14-15**, 20-22
    headquarters/offices, 16, 17, **17**, 20, **20**, 30, **30**
    name change, 39, 89
    125th anniversary event, 15, **15**
    tagline/logo, 34, **34**, 89

Consumers Energy Foundation, 60

Consumers Power Company. *See* Consumers Energy Company (formerly Consumers Power Company)

Consumers Power Foundation, 142

Cook, James, 64

Cooke hydroelectric plant, 29, 50

Coopersville Muldoons, 51

Correct RoadsidE ProtEction Saves Lives (CREEL), 115

Crain's Detroit Business, 10, 146

Creel, Jeffery, 115

Cross Winds Energy Park, 120, **120**, 140

Croton hydroelectric plant, **24-25**, 25-27, 50-51

Customer Choice and Electricity Reliability Act, 95

customer service/satisfaction, 13-16, 71, 73, 94, 103, 108, 114, 116, **117-118**, 123, 128, 129, 131, 134, 145-149

D

Daly, Kip, 134, 136

dams. *See* hydroelectric plants

Dansville, Michigan, 30-32

Davis, Howard, 36

Dawson, Gary, 75

D.E. Karn fossil-fuel plant, 36, 45, 54, 140. *See also* Karn-Weadock fossil-fuel complex

Dearborn Industrial Generation (DIG) facility, 89

Dearborn, Michigan, 83, 103

Decontamination for Decommissioning, 92

deregulation, 82, 94-95, 98, 116

Detroit City Gas, 38

Detroit Edison (DTE Energy), 11, 13, 48, 59, 82

Detroit, Michigan, 34, 39, 59, 61, 64, 75

Detroit River International Wildlife Refuge, 75

Dillon, Pat, 133, **133**, 147

distribution, 71, 89, 98, 112, 128, 149

Dormant wanigan, 26

Dow Chemical USA, 57, 60, 61, 64, 66, 68, 69

Duke Energy, 82

Dynegy, 98

E

East Park, 111

Ecuador, 84, **85**, 87

Edison Electric Institute's Index Award, 16

Edison, Thomas Alva, 17

Eisenhower, Dwight D., 36

Elbert, Paul, 38, 39, 59, 73, 74, 76, 77

Electric Customer Choice program, 95

Electric Light and Power magazine, 77

Electric Railway Securities Company, 31

electricity, 16-18, 20-22, 24, 25, 29. *See also* rural electrification

Elward, Tom, 54, 57-59, 97, 106

Employee Resource Groups, 72

employees, 17, 25, 30, **30**, 32, 59, 60, **60**, 69, **69**, **70**, 71-77, **75**, 89, **89**, 92, **92**, **102**, 103-106, 108, **109**, 114, 115, 123, 126-129, **130-131**, 131, **138**, 139, 141-143, **141-143**, 145-149, **146-149**

Empresa Distribuidora de Electricidad de Entre Rios (EDEERSA), 80, 84, 87

Energy Policy Act (1992), 84

Engler, John, 95

English, Carl, 39, 66, 68, 99

Enhanced Infrastructure Replacement Project (EIRP), 71, **71**

Enron, 99

Ensenada, cogeneration project in, 84

Entergy, 82

Entergy Nuclear Palisades, LLC, 94

environment, 16, 54, 74-75, **74-75**, 89, 92, 95, 110-113, 116, 119, 123, 128, 134, 136, 140, **140**, 141, 147

Equatorial Guinea, 87, 108

Erwin, George, 25-26

Ettawageshik, Frank, 113

Evergreen Utility and Telecommunications Fund, 106

F

Fargo, William, 26, **26**, 51

farming, 90-91, **90-91**, 149

Federal Energy Regulatory Commission (FERC), 83, 84

Fermi 2 nuclear plant, 59

financial status, 25, 30, 32, 59, 73, 77, 87, 96, 98, 99, 103-108, 112-113, 127, 128, **128**, 142, 143, 145, 148. *See also* bankruptcy

FIRST, 142

Five Channels hydroelectric plant, 29, 50, 51, **51**

Flint, Michigan, 34, 132, 142

Foote hydroelectric plant, 29

Foote Hospital (now Henry Ford Allegiance Health), 142

Foote, Ida, 142

Foote, James Berry ("J.B."), 14, 17, 20-21, **20**, 23-27, 29, 30, 50, 51, 149

Foote, William Augustine ("W.A."), 12, 14, 17, 20, **20**, 22-27, 29, 30, 50, 51, 142, 149

Ford, Gerald, 61, 82

Ford, Richard, 60, 114

fossil-fuel power, 13, 16, 36, 45, 54, 59, 69, 73, 74, 75, 77, 84, 89. *See also* coal/coal power, natural gas, oil/oil power *and specific plant names*

Fowler, Michigan, 90

Frankfort, Michigan, 90

Franklin, Benjamin, 29

Fryling, Vic, 82, 97

Future Builders, 25

Future Farmers of America, 91

G

Garrity, Bill, 118

Gas Customer Choice program, 95

General Electric, 20, 22, 27, 37

General Motors, 60, 75, 114

generation, 34, **34-35**, 95, 98, 126, 136

generators, 16, 20, 21, 22-23, 51, 66, 84

Genesee County, 136

geothermal power, 134

Gilbert/Commonwealth, 15

GMR Vasavi, 86, **86**

Grand Rapids Gas Light Company, 27

Grand Rapids, Michigan, 20, 23, 25-27, **27**, 48, 51, 142

Grand Rapids-Muskegon Water Power Electric Company, 26

Grand River, 23, 26, 50

Grand Valley State University, 120, **120-121**, 134, **135**, 140

Granholm, Jennifer, 120

Grayling Generating Station, 134, **134**

Grayling, Michigan, 133

Greenville, Michigan, 133

Griesbach, Fern, 73, 145, 146

Groveland Customer Service Center, 133

GSO Capital Partners LP, 73

Gulf of Mexico, 106, **106**

GVK Industries plant, 86

H

Habitant wanigan, 26

Habitat for Humanity, 142, **142**

Hampton Township, 45, 140

Handley-Brown water heater, 30

Handley, William, Sr., 30

Hardy, George E., 30

Hardy hydroelectric plant, 27, 30, 51

Harris, Kevin, **14**, 15

Harris, Laurie (Barrett), 14-15, **14**

Harris, Tyler, **14**, 15

Hausler, Lee, 92

"Headstart on Tomorrow," 40

Health Department of Northern Michigan, 111

Henry Ford Allegiance Health, 142

Hidroelectrica El Chocon, 80, **80-81**

Hispanic Outreach Team, 72

Hodenpyl, Anton G., 27, 30

Hodenpyl-Walbridge & Company, 27, 29, 30

Holland, Michigan, 13, 36, 142

Homer, Michigan, 133

Hotel Lawrence, 23, **23**

Howell natural gas field, 12, **12-13**

Hudson River Power Transmission Company, 29

Hutchinson, John, 13

Hydro Hall of Fame, 51

hydroelectric power, 11, 13, 16, 18, 20-27, **26**, 29, **31**, 48, 50-51, 75, 80, 84, 134, 136. *See also specific plant names*

I

independent power producers (IPPs), 83, 84

India, 78, 86, **86**, 99

Indonesia, 87

international business, 78, **78-79**, 80, 82-84, **84-86**, 86-87, 89, 94, 96-99, 106, 143

Interprovincial-Lakehead pipeline, 52

Ira Township, **136-137**

Izzo, Tom, 128

J

Jackson Common Council, 23-24

Jackson County, 143

Jackson Electric Light and Power Company, 23

Jackson Electric Light Works, 16, 21, **21**, 24

Jackson, Michigan, 12, 15, 16, 17, **17**, 20, 23-27, **23**, 29, 31, 34, 58, 60, 69, **69**, 102, 103, 136, 142, 147, 148

Jamaica, 78

Jarvis, Samuel, 17, 23, 24

J.C. Weadock fossil-fuel plant, 13, 17, 34, 36, **44-45**, 45, 140, 141. *See also* Karn-Weadock fossil-fuel complex

J.D. Power's customer satisfaction survey, 16

J.H. Campbell fossil-fuel plant, 13, 36, 45, 54, 76, 112, 126, **126**, 140

Johnson, David, 110

Johnson, Frank, 58, 59, 80, **80**, 84, 86, 87, 97, 98, 126
Joos, Dave, 38, 57-59, **58**, 83, 93, 98, 105, 108, 112, **112**, 113, 123, 127
Jorf Lasfar plant (Morocco), 78, 96, 108, **108**
J.R. Whiting fossil-fuel plant, 13, 16, **16**, 36, 45, **46-47**, 47, 75, **75**, 89, 92, 112, 140, 141, 147

K

Kalamazoo, Michigan, 20-22, 25, 27, 30, 71, 140
Kalamazoo River, 20, 25
Kalamazoo River Generating Station, **88**, 89
Karn, Daniel, 34, 36, 37
Karn-Weadock fossil-fuel complex, 13, 73, 74-75, 76, 77, 112, 114, 119. *See also* D.E. Karn fossil-fuel plant *and* J.C. Weadock fossil-fuel plant
Kenney, Timothy A., 29, 32
Kessler, Bill, 15, **15**
Kids Food Basket, 142
kitchen, traveling, 36, **36**
Kloack, Coley, **14**, 15
Kloack, Kris, **14**
Kloack, Teresa, **14**

L

Lake Erie, 13, 75, **75**, 89
Lake Michigan, 11, 13, 37, 41, 48, 110, 113, 126
Lake Winds Energy Park, 75, 124, **124-125**, 138-140, **138-139**
landfill gas power, 134
Lansing Fuel and Gas, 30
Lansing, Michigan, 23, 48, 64, 90, 147
Latin America, 87
Lehman, Pete, 66, **66**, 68
"Let's DOET Tour," 149
Levin, Carl, 68
Little Traverse Bay, 110
LO NOx burners, 92
Loe, Andy, 94, **94**
Loud, Edward, 26, **26**, 29
Loud hydroelectric plant, 29, 50
Loy Yang A plant, 97
Ludington Mariners, 51
Ludington, Michigan, 48, 54
Ludington Pumped Storage Facility, 8, **8-9**, 11, 13, 16, 45, 48-50, **48-49**, 54, 112, 136-138
Luna Pier, Michigan, 140
Lupo, Debbie, 17

M

Malone, Dan, 115, 132, 133
Manistee County, 140
Manistee River, 51, 75
manufactured/synthetic gas, 32, 49, 52-54
Marathon, 106
Marcellus basin (Pennsylvania), 134

Margarita Island, 98
Marshall Training Center, 15, 120, **122**, 123, 146-147
Martin & Giddings, 23, **23**
Marvin, Dennis, 138
Marysville Gas Reforming Plant, 52-54, **52-53**
Marysville, Michigan, 49
Mason County, 75, 140
Mason-Dansville line, 30-32, **32**, 90
Mason, Michigan, 30-31, 32
McAndrews, Phil, 94, 99, 106
McCormick, William ("Bill"), 61, **61**, 64, 66, **66**, 68, 72, 73, 80, 82, 83, 87, 98, **98**, 99, 102
Mengebier, David, 123
Metropolitan Edison, 58
Michigan, as service area, 11, 13, 16, 29, 34, **34**
Michigan Audubon Society, 74
Michigan Department of Environmental Quality, 89
Michigan Department of Natural Resources Wetland Wonders Challenge, 75
Michigan Economic Development Corporation, 132
Michigan Light Company, 27, 30
Michigan Public Service Commission (MPSC), 59, 60, 68, 69, 72, 83, 84, 94, 95, 99, 113, 116
Michigan State University, 90
Michigan State Utility Workers Council, 133, 147
Michigan Trust Company, 27
Middle East, 96, 99
Midland Cogeneration Venture (MCV), 42, 62-69, 62, **62-63**, 64-69, **64-65**, **66**, **67**, **68**, 72-73, 77, **77**, 82, 83, 84
Midland, Michigan, 56
Midland Nuclear Plant, 15, 42, **42-43**, 56-61, **56**, **60**, 64
Midwest Independent Transmission System Operator (MISO), 13
Mierzwa, Terence, 38, 39
Minority Advisory Panel, 72
Mio hydroelectric plant, 29, 50
Mitchell-Reid Company, 23
mobile-responsive website, 131, **131**
Moody's Investor Services, 108
Moran Iron Works, 132, **132**
Morgan, J. P., 17
Morocco, 89, 96, 106, 108, **108**
Morris, Mike, 72, 89
Muskegon, Michigan, 25, 36, 51, 140-141, 142
Muskegon River, 25-27, 30, 50, 51, 75

N

National Incident Management System (NIMS), 114
National Safety Council, 77
natural gas, 12, 16, 17, 30, 32, 34, 36, 38-39, **38**, 49, 50, 52, 57, 61, 66, 69, 71-73, 82-84, 87, 89, **89**, 97, 98, 106, 112, 118-120, 134, 136, 140, 148, 149. *See also specific plant names*
Netherland, Matthew, 75
New Hampshire, 99

New South Wales, 97

New York, 95

New York Stock Exchange, 38, 82, 123, **123**

New Zealand, 87

North America, 89

Northern Michigan Exploration Company (NOMECO), 36, 83, 87

Nuclear Management Company (NMC), 93-94

nuclear power, 13, 15, 16, 36-37, 40, 41, 42, 54-61, 62, 64, 66, 68, 92-94, 95, 112, 113, 148. *See also specific plant names*

Nuclear Regulatory Commission (NRC), 55, 57-59, 93

O

Oakland County, 38, 133

O'Brien, Timothy, 106

Odawa Native Americans, 37, 113

Ohio, 134

oil/oil power, 16, 36, 52, 61, 69, 83, 84, 87, 89, 98, 106, 136, 148. *See also specific plant names*

Otsego Dam, 25

Owendale, Michigan, 90

P

Palisades Nuclear Plant, 13, 41, 54-57, **54-55**, 93-95, **95**, 112

Panhandle Eastern pipeline, 34, 36

Panhandle Trunkline, 106

Peck, Ralph Brazelton, 57

Pennsylvania, 134

PeopleCare program, 143

Pere Marquette River, 48

Petoskey, Michigan, 110, 111

Petrosky, Tim, 92

Philippines, 78, 87

pipelines, 71, 89, 98, 106, **106**, 112. *See also specific pipeline names*

Plainwell Dam, 25

Pontiac, Michigan, 27, 34

Poppe, Patti, 15, **15**, 71, 129, 146, **146**, 148-149

Power Plant and Industrial Fuel Use Act, 69

Powering a Generation of Change, 87

Powers, William, 23

Preketees, Paul, 114

Public Service Electric & Gas, 114

Public Utilities Regulatory Policy Act of 1978 (PURPA), 69

Public Utility Holding Company Act (PUHCA), 34, 83, 94

Pure Michigan Business Connect Initiative, **132**, 133

Q

Qualifying Facilities (QFs), 69

R

Rand, Frank, 147

Rasmussen, Ronn, 113

Reagan, Ronald, 40, **41**, 82

reliability, 16, 45, 71, 73, 77, 94, 95, 108, 112, 114, 123, 128, 131, 134, 136, 145, 147

Reliant Resources, 98

renewable energy, 120, 123, 126, 134, 138, 148

reservoirs, 49, 50

Riverton Township, 138

Rochow, Garrick, 128, 131, 133

Rockland Capital Energy, 73

Rofan Energy Inc., 68

Rogers hydroelectric plant, 26, 27, 50, 51

Roosevelt, Franklin D., 34

Rouge Education Project, 75

Rouge River, 75

round-trip trading, 98-99

rural electrification, 30-32, **32**, 36. *See also* farming

Russell, John, 13, 15, 16, 39, 75, 115, 123, **123**, 126-128, **126-127**, 133, **133**, 141, 145, 146, 148

Russia, 36-37

S

safety, 16, 17, 39, 57, 73, 77, 92, **92**, 93, 112, 114-115, **114-115**, 123, 128, 131, 136, 146, 147

Safety Culture Transition Team, 115

Saginaw Bay, 36, 74

Saginaw Bay Watershed Initiative Network, 142

Saginaw, Michigan, 27, 31, 32

Saginaw River, 13

Saginaw River steam generating plant, 30, 31, **31**

Salvation Army, 143

Sanders, W.K., 106, **107**

Schoenlein, Bill, 11, 13, 16, 48, 136

Schroeder, Richard, 90

Securities and Exchange Commission, 94, 99

Selby, John, 57, 59, 60

shareholders, 16, 45, 60, 77, 82, 83, 98, **98**, 99, 108, **109**

Shuweihat S1 plant, 96

Simpson, John, 49

Sinclair, Mary, 57, **57**

Smithsonian Institution, 87

Sniegowski, Michael, 111

Snyder, Lauren Youngdahl, 15, **15**

Solar Gardens power plants, 120, **120-121**, 134, **135**

solar power, 50, 123, 120, 140, 126, 134, 140. *See also* Solar Gardens power plants

South America, 80, 84, 97, 99, 108

South Haven, Michigan, 41

Southeastern Power & Light Company, 31

Southern Michigan Light and Power, 30

Southern Union Panhandle Corp., 106

Southwest Michigan Pipeline, 39, **39**

Sparks, Tim, 140, 141

St. Clair Compressor Station, 136, **136-137**

steam generating plants, 29, 30, 31, 36, 64- 69, 73, 89. *See also specific plant names*
Stecker, George, 20-21, 25, 30, 51
Steinmetz, Charles, 27
stock, 73, 77, 82, 83, **83**, 89, 94, 99, 103, 106, 108, 112, 123
Stop the Job Campaign, 147
store, company, 147
storms, **70**, 71
strategic business units (SBUs), 38, 39
Strauss, Lewis, 37
street lighting, 22-24, **22**, 27, **27**
Summit Township, 138
Suppliers Summits, 132-133
sustainability, 16, 123

T

technology, 89, 92, 119, 120, 128, 129, **129**, 134, 136
Terra Energy Ltd., 87, **87**
Thailand, 87
Thelen, Gerald, 90
Thetford, Michigan, 136
Thomson-Houston Electric Company, 22
Thomson-Houston generator, 23
Thornapple Gas and Electric, 30
Three Mile Island Nuclear Generating Station (Pennsylvania), 58
Tippy, Charles W., 30-32, 34
Tippy hydroelectric plant, 51, 75
Tittawabassee River, 57, 66
Toshiba, 137
Trail Street steam plant, 29
trainers, 115
Trans-Elect, 95-96
transmission, 32, **33**, 34, **34-35**, 50, 83, 84, 89, 95-96, 98, 105, **105**, 138, 149
TriMars compressor station, 106, **106**
Trowbridge hydroelectric project, 18, **18-19**, 20-21, 25
Trowbridge, Michigan, 20
Trunkline-Consumers Power system, 36
Trunkline distribution system, 106
Trunkline Gas Co., 106
Tunisia, 87
turbines, 13, 20, 26, **46-47**, 47-49, 51, 66, 136-139, **138**
Turkey, 97
Tuscola County, 140
21st Century Electric Energy Plan, 116

U

unions, 15, 73, 74, 76, 84, 108, 114, 115, 127, 146, 147
United Arab Emirates, 96
United Way, 143
U.S. Atomic Energy Commission, 37
U.S. Department of Energy, 72
U.S. electric power industry, 27
U.S. energy policy, 16
U.S. Nuclear Regulatory Commission, 93

Utica basin (Pennsylvania), 134
Utility Workers Union of America (UWUA), 76, 115, 146
Utility Working Group, 83

V

Van Buren County, 41
Van Slooten, Steve, 108, 115
vehicles (company), 27, **27**, 29, **29**, 36, **36**, **71**, 90, **90**, **114**, **130**, 131, **145**, **148-149**
Venezuela, 97, 98
Veterans Advisory Panel, 72
Vogel, Ted, 45, 52, 69
Volunteer Investment Program (VIP), 143
Voyageur wanigan, 26

W

Walbridge, Henry D., 27, 30
Walk for Warmth, 143, **143**
wanigans, 26, **26**
Warner, Shad, **14**
Wawro, Stephen, 119
Weadock, J.C., **26**
Webb, Tom, 104-106, **104**, 108
Webber hydroelectric plant, 26, 50, **50**
Weekly Plus, 89
West Olive, Michigan, 76
Western Michigan University, 140
Westinghouse, 15
Whipple, Ken, 102-106, **102**, 108, **109**, 112, 127, 143
White Pigeon, Michigan, 106
Wildlife Habitat Council, 75
Williams, G. Mennen, 106, **107**
Willkie, Wendell, 32, 34
wind power, 50, 75, 120, **120**, 123, 124, **124-125**, 126, 134, 138, **138-139**, 140. *See also specific plant names*
Women's Advisory Panel, 72, **72**
Women's Engineering Network, 72
Wyss, Alfred, 51

Y

Yasinsky, John, 98, 108
Youngdahl, Lauren. *See* Snyder, Lauren Youngdahl
Youngdahl, Leslie, 15, **15**
Youngdahl, Neil, 15, **15**
Youngdahl, Russell, Sr., 15, **15**, 41, 57

Z

Zeeland combined-cycle generating facility, 118, 119, **119**
Zilwaukee transmission line, **28**, 29
Zilwaukee, Michigan, 31